DEM●S

Demos is an independent think tank committed to radical thinking on the long-term problems facing the UK and other advanced industrial societies.

It aims to develop ideas – both theoretical and practical – to help shape the politics of the twenty first century, and to improve the breadth and quality of political debate.

Demos publishes books and a regular journal and undertakes substantial empirical and policy oriented research projects. Demos is a registered charity.

In all its work Demos brings together people from a wide range of backgrounds in business, academia, government, the voluntary sector and the media to share and cross-fertilise ideas and experiences.

For further information and
subscription details please contact:
Demos
Panton House
25 Haymarket
London SW1Y 4EN
Telephone: 0171 321 2200
Facsimile: 0171 321 2342
email: mail@demos.co.uk

Other publications available from Demos:

Access Denied: Preventing information exclusion

*The Employee Mutual: Stability and security in
the new world of work*

Governing in the Round: Strategies for holistic government

To Our Mutual Advantage

An inclusive future?

Disability, social change and opportunities for greater inclusion by 2010

Ian Christie with Gavin Mensah-Coker

First published in 1999 by
Demos
Panton House
25 Haymarket
London SW1Y 4EN
Telephone: 0171 321 2200
Facsimile: 0171 321 2342
email: mail@demos.co.uk

ISBN 1 84180 000 7
Printed in Great Britain by Redwood Books, Trowbridge
Design by Lindsay Nash

Contents

Acknowledgements

The authors are grateful to the NDC for commissioning and sponsoring the study and to the DfEE for its administrative and research support. We have benefited greatly from the advice, constructive criticism and information supplied by the members of the Steering Committee and Advisory Group which oversaw the process of designing the NDC symposium and this report. We are most grateful for the advice and encouragement we have received, and for the time members of the two groups generously dedicated to the project. We have also had sterling assistance from Leonard Cheshire, which hosted meetings of the Steering Committee and Advisory Group and also provided access to its latest qualitative research, carried out by Opinion Leader Research, on the social exclusion of disabled people. We are grateful to David Grayson and Bert Massie of NDC, Tom Bentley, Mike Floyd, Sally French and Marilyn Howard for helpful comments on the drafts of the report. Finally, we would like to thank all those who took part in the NDC symposium which helped to shape the report; Debbie Porter and her team who organised the event; and Lindsay Nash who prepared the report for publication.

Members of the Steering Committee and Advisory Group are:

Doug Alker, Rob Banks, Nita Bhupal, Helen Bolderson, Kevin Carey, Gordon Dryden, Dick Edwards, Ruth Geall, Angelika Hibbett, John Knight, Brian Lamb, Colin Low, Paul Macmillan, Alice Maynard-Lupton, Susan Scott-Parker, Sue Sharp, Gavin Smart, Patricia Thornton, Richard Timm and Gerry Zarb.

The ideas expressed in the report are the responsibility of the authors and should not be assumed to represent the views of any of the individuals or organisations which have informed or supported our study.

Foreword

This important report from Demos for the National Disability Council (NDC) raises a number of challenges for disability rights campaigners generally and for the forthcoming Disability Rights Commission in particular. We are very grateful to Leonard Cheshire for agreeing to fund a research project, focusing on opinion formers' views on disability policy issues of social inclusion for disabled people, which is drawn on in the report.[1]

Three key challenges stand out. First, the need to be **future-alert**: acutely aware of the major trends in technology, social attitudes and values, governance and business – and how these trends might affect disabled people.

> *For example* – a vocal and well-organised disability lobby would be a powerful force compelling candidates for mayor of London (and subsequently, other cities) to articulate disabled-friendly policies if they want the votes of disabled people.

Second, disability organisations and campaigners are going to need to **broaden horizons**: to think not just about conventional 'disability questions', but to intervene actively in the national debates about housing policy, urban regeneration and lifetime learning.

> *For example* – disability organisations could help those developing new learning institutions, like the University for Industry, understand better the need to design in from the start access for disabled people, and could provide practical suggestions for doing so.

And third, disability rights campaigners will have to build **strategic alliances** and become expert advisers and partners to a range of other sectors.

> *For example* – in debates about the revitalisation of town centres, local disability access committees might make common cause with town centre managers, architects and planners to promote their locality as being 'disabled friendly'.

We cannot afford to keep to our own territory or comfort zones! We must all be outward-looking and forward-thinking. For disability organisations and campaigners, this lesson is underlined by experiences like our failure to engage with business arguments and convince government that the Disability Discrimination Act's employment threshold should have been significantly reduced.

None of this is to underplay the significance of more legally enforceable rights for disabled people, but as the Demos report makes clear, how quickly the rights of disabled people are comprehensively realised will depend in large measure on how far we succeed in influencing a whole series of other policy areas. 'Joined-up' thinking is as important for disabled people and our organisations as it is for government.

The NDC is delighted, therefore, to be working with Demos as part of our 'Paving the Way for the DRC' programme.

David Grayson
Chairman, National Disability Council

Summary of key points

- The systematic disadvantage experienced by many disabled people has been challenged and tackled through many initiatives in recent years, but equal rights and genuine 'inclusion' remain to be achieved. A major opportunity to achieve greater equality and inclusion **could** be provided by the large-scale **modernisation** which will be seen in the UK in the next two decades. The overhaul of the UK's policies and infrastructures for work, welfare, learning and communications opens up opportunities for 'designing in' equality of access and opportunity for disabled people **from the outset** in the reinvention of organisations, services and systems.

- The changing age profile of the population means that a greater proportion of citizens will have some direct or indirect experience of disability. As a result the political importance of disability issues is likely to rise.

- In the worlds of **work and learning**, economic, technological and organisational changes will be profound, breaking down old barriers between sectors and services. Insecurities in work are intensifying for many: these could be countered by innovations in labour market and educational bodies and systems, especially through new forms of **mutual organisation** which could especially benefit disabled people.

- In relation to **citizenship**, innovations potentially benefiting disabled people are as follows: Legal – the introduction of new rights via the

DDA and the Disability Rights Commission; Political – new scope for participation in the reformed UK constitutional landscape; Social and Cultural – new opportunities from the flood of information and communication systems now emerging; Economic – innovations possible as the reform of the benefits system proceeds and if a concept of citizenship based on **mutualism** is developed.

● In the field of **'design for life'**, the regeneration of the physical fabric of housing, urban areas, communications and public transport offers new opportunities – again, based on a principle of mutual benefit – to improve disability access and recognition of disabled people's needs and expertise. The same is true of the design of new domestic technologies.

● In all these areas there are risks of continued marginalisation and exclusion as well as opportunities for genuine progress to inclusion. Nothing is guaranteed: but the scope for engagement on many fronts with a far-reaching set of modernisation processes is immense and the opportunities for greater inclusion are real.

Introduction

This report is a revised version of a paper prepared for the participants in the National Disability Council (NDC) Symposium *An Inclusive Future*, held at the Business Design Centre in London on 29 April 1999. The aim of this event was to bring together disabled and non-disabled people – campaigners, researchers, service providers, business people, policy-makers – in order to think creatively about ways in which genuine progress can be made in the coming decade to overcome the barriers that affect the rights and quality of life of people facing disabling barriers.

The report is based on a review of recent research on disability, work and inclusion/exclusion of disabled people; interviews with experts from disability organisations and from the research and consulting worlds; and informal brainstorming on links between major societal trends and the prospects for greater inclusion of disabled people in society.

No attempt is made here to provide a comprehensive study of every aspect of social exclusion and every possibility for greater social inclusion affecting disabled people. The aim is to highlight some of the main changes we can reasonably expect to see in society over the next ten to fifteen years, to identify new opportunities where they exist, and to consider ways in which existing prejudice, ignorance and structural barriers to inclusion might be overcome.

The thrust of the report is that the process of 'modernisation' in many walks of life, driven variously by government policy on welfare, devolution, public services and learning, by globalisation, by business innovation in IT and by large-scale pressures of demographic and environmental change, opens up major opportunities for disabled people. The scale of *restructuring and new design* in society – organisational, technological and environmental – over the next ten years and more brings opportunities for positive change for disabled people. The establishment of new processes and institutions in principle makes it possible to 'design in' disability awareness and equal access from the outset.

Moreover, the process of 'modernisation' across sectors not only highlights new possibilities but also exposes barriers to necessary change in a sharper light. Failures by particular interests to meet new challenges and deal with old ones – such as systematic discrimination – can be seen as symptomatic of wider problems of adaptation to the modern world. Dealing with discrimination, for example, can be advocated not only as a moral and legal requirement but also as an essential aspect of making a service or an organisational culture fit for purpose in the operating environment of the new century.

Thus, despite our proper awareness of the enormity of the problems faced by many disabled people and by carers, and of the huge outstanding task of improving day-to-day conditions in the short term, if we look at a longer time-scale we can see big opportunities opening up. This is especially the case in relation to information and communication technologies, which could, *if supported by suitable policies and attitudes*, play a major role in promoting equality and inclusive citizenship. Underpinning initiatives to make the most of these opportunities will be a form of *mutuality*. This means a recognition of the mutual interests of disabled and non-disabled people; of the interdependence of rights and responsibilities; and of the ways in which achieving genuine social and economic inclusion for disabled people *can be of benefit to the non-disabled population as well as desirable and just in its own right*.

The 'modernisation project' and new interest in mutuality will not deliver a more inclusive future for disabled people 'automatically'. What they provide is a fruitful set of opportunities which need to be seized. This will depend on determined campaigning, political willpower, a commitment to 'joined up' thinking and action at all levels of government and business, full implementation of legislation on disability equality, and the creation of new alliances and partnerships for change between disabled people's organisations and other groups concerned with social inclusion and equal rights. *Nothing is guaranteed;*

but much potential is there to be exploited – indeed, the scope for progress is unprecedented if we have the will to act on the possibilities to create a truly inclusive society.

Outline of the report

The structure of the report is as follows. The rest of this introduction outlines the context for the research and the NDC/Demos symposium in April 1999, and considers the fundamental features of the deep-seated problems of social exclusion faced by disabled people. It also reflects briefly on the models of understanding of disability which have been the focus for campaigning and much debate in recent years. It suggests that the nature of the debates and campaigns engaged in by disability organisations could change significantly in the next two decades as powerful forces promote social change in these key areas:

- work and learning
- citizenship
- 'design for life': technology and the built environment.

Chapter 1 focuses on the routes to 'inclusion' at the heart of current government policy and long-term vision – **work and learning**. It outlines some of what we know about the employment experiences of disabled people and considers the opportunities and potential problems ahead from likely changes in the world of work. (A more detailed, though far from exhaustive, review of recent research is provided in the appendix.)

In relation to learning, the chapter looks at the idea of a 'learning society' and what opportunities and potential problems this throws up for disabled people. It also considers the learning that needs to be done by the non-disabled population before we can say that disabled people have been properly 'included' as equal citizens.

Chapter 2 considers the idea of **citizenship**, a fundamental element in any meaningful notion of 'social inclusion'. We consider changing views of citizenship and the tensions arising in current policy approaches. Four issues are highlighted: first, the impact of the Disability Rights Commission (DRC); second, the impact of new interactive information systems and digital television; third, the growth in opportunities for democratic participation; and fourth, the benefits system.

Chapter 3 picks up themes from the previous discussion in considering **'design for life'** – the potential of new technologies in information systems, disability aids and home design. It also looks at the scope for overcoming the extreme exclusion for disabled people caused by poor design in the built environment, including the public transport system.

Each chapter ends with a summary of key recommendations.

Disability: the present context for policy

The past 30 years have seen disability rights campaigners carve out a significant place in public debate. Forms of compensation and support for disabled people have been part of the welfare policy agenda throughout the century, with an impetus provided by the impact of the First World War[2] and by the establishment of the post-Second World War welfare state.[3] But it was only in the 1960s and 1970s that arguments from disabled people and advocacy organisations began to pose powerful challenges to the definition of capacities and needs underpinning policies on disability. These were based on the emerging failures of welfare policy to overcome exclusion among disabled people, on the defects of a medical definition of disabled people's condition of disadvantage, and on the need for a rights-based approach to combat discrimination.[4]

Since then disability rights campaigners have emerged as one of the most trenchant lobby groups in society, as witnessed in the debates surrounding the implementation of the 1995 Disability Discrimination Act (DDA). This act provides protection for disabled people at work and, with the further implementation of Part III of the Act from October 1999, will also seek to ensure that disabled people can play a full role as consumers in the market place.

Basic statistics about disability

Disability is a contested, complex idea. It covers a wide spectrum of medically defined impairments and the social, environmental and economic obstacles to full enjoyment of 'social inclusion' that are associated with them. Impairments linked to 'disability' range from severe to minor constraints on mobility, sight, hearing, speech and learning, and include mental illnesses as well as physical conditions. Measurement of the population of people with impairments is not straightforward. Estimates vary considerably, depending on whether an official definition or self-definition is used in surveys, on what kind of sampling is done and on what models of disability are used in defining the sample and the questions. So we should *expect* considerable variation in results between surveys, no matter how rigorously designed they are.

But while this inevitable imprecision in counting 'the disabled' is an issue for researchers, it has its value: it reminds us of the blurred boundary between disabled and non-disabled people, of the continuum that exists and which – as we argue in what follows – could be seen as a positive underpinning to policies for social inclusion for disabled people in future. And it is important to note that although the exact figure depends on the definitions and questions used, this makes no difference to the fact that however we make the measurement, disabled people make up a significant proportion of the population in the UK.

Latest government data from the Labour Force Survey (LFS) for spring 1999 suggest that disabled people account for nearly one-fifth of the working-age population in Great Britain: over 6.3 million people have 'a current long-term disability or health problem that has a substantial adverse impact on their day-to-day activities or limits the work they can do'.[5] The DfEE estimates that there are 8.7 million people in the UK of all ages with a current disability who are covered by the Disability Discrimination Act; there are 2.9 million disabled people in employment, and they make up 11 per cent of all people in employment.[6] Using a different set of definitions, and covering a wider age range than the LFS, the 1998 Disability Follow-up Survey suggests there are 8.6 million disabled adults.[7] But the key point is this: whatever the definition used, the total disabled population is very large – we are not discussing a small minority group. In addition, there are nearly 6 million carers for people with a long-term impairment or long-term illness, and these are famously estimated to provide services that would, if provided by the State, cost over £30 billion per annum.

LFS data show that unemployment is higher among disabled people than among the non-disabled, and that over a million of those who are currently inactive want to work. There are over 2.6 million disabled people out of work and claiming benefits.[8] Disabled people are only half as likely as non-disabled people to be in employment, and are more than twice as likely to have no formal qualifications.[9] The DfEE survey by Meager et al shows that disabled workers are more likely to work in manual and lower-skilled occupations, and less likely to be found in managerial, professional and higher-skilled work.[10] This study also shows that disabled people from ethnic minorities are more likely to be unemployed than are their white counterparts. Employment rates vary a great deal by type of disability: people with mental illness and learning disabilities, for example, are far less likely to be in work than are people with hearing problems, diabetes and skin conditions. There is consistent reporting of discrimination:[11] in one of the most comprehensive and informative recent surveys, while most disabled respondents reported being broadly content with their recent experience of work and the way they had been treated, 16 per cent said they had been discriminated against by an employer or potential employer.[12]

In work, disabled people's earnings are low compared to those of the non-disabled: 58 per cent of disabled people earn less than £10,000 per annum compared to the 30 per cent national average, whereas only 13 per cent earn above £20,000 compared to the 39 per cent national average.[13] The DfEE's large national interview survey by IES and NOP on disabled people's participation in the workforce found that on average disabled employees have lower take-home pay (£196 per week) compared to non-disabled employees (£212 per week).[14] Disabled people are in addition more likely than the non-disabled to live in public housing – 45 per cent are council tenants or housing association tenants compared to 31 per cent of the general population.[15]

The appended review of statistics on disability and recent research on the employment issues relating to disabled people underlines the many forms of disadvantage facing them.

New directions in policy

The present Labour government has committed itself to tackling 'social exclusion' through a 'joined-up' approach to policy-making and implementation. Exclusion means exposure to long-term problems which cut people off from 'mainstream' opportunities for work, learning, a decent quality of life and participation in civic life. These include long-term unemployment, persistent poverty, systematic discrimination, home-lessness, exclusion from school, criminal activity, and so on. The solu-tions to such problems cannot rely on the work of a single agency or policy: cross-functional and cross-agency working is vital.

The government is setting up a Disability Rights Commission (DRC), which will have similar functions to the Commission for Racial Equality and the Equal Opportunities Commission. The DRC starts work in 2000. The government has also given impetus to existing schemes for improving employment for disabled people, such as Access to Work (financial support for disabled people to assist, for example, with adjustments, with providing special equipment and with the cost of fares to work). It has included disabled people as a target group in the New Deal package for assisting unemployed people from welfare into work, training or education.

Steps are being taken to consider the issues facing people with disabilities in a 'joined-up' way, seeking to overcome the many problems and inconsistencies stemming from the traditional fragmentation of policies concerned separately with employment, benefits and rights.[16] A truly integrated approach is some way off yet, but the establishment of the DRC, the New Deal for Disabled People, and the new unified 'work-focused gateway' service (dubbed 'One') for all benefit claimants, is significant. Other steps which should simplify what has been a frag-mented and dauntingly complex system for access to employment opportunities, personal social services and benefits include:

- a pilot personal advisor service in twelve areas;
- improved co-ordination between central and local government and the NHS;
- a strategy to improve support for carers of people with disabilities, including the introduction of new second pensions for carers, improved respite care provision, initiatives to help carers find paid work, plans for helping school-age carers, and scope for local authorities to provide new support to carers.

Much depends on the extent to which the budgets, political will and skills are in place to implement these joined-up policies well. Local authorities are likely to respond to the overall strategy in very differ-

ent ways, and some developments threaten to *worsen* exclusion for many
disabled people. In many areas social services budgets for carers and
disabled people's services are being cut and/or charges for services are
being introduced. And some people with disabilities are having their
benefits reduced as part of welfare reform. In addition, it remains to
be seen how effective the New Deal for Disabled People will be in getting
its clients into jobs that meet their needs, and how far the principle that
all who can work should seek it, now a basic theme in benefits policy,
will be suitable for many disabled people.

The new wave of policies, for all their limitations, underlines that
progress has undeniably been made in raising awareness of the barriers to full civil rights and social inclusion experienced by many disabled
people. The justified anger of many disability campaigners in the face
of barriers to social inclusion has fuelled a sustained period of research,
protest, lobbying and policy proposals which have achieved major
changes in legislation and outlook. For all the fundamental changes still
to be made before disabling barriers to 'inclusion' are overcome, the
establishment of the DDA and the DRC reflect a major change in the
social climate. The deliberate social exclusion of disabled people is no
longer a tolerable public position for organisations. If public opinion
condemns prejudice towards disabled people then there is an opportunity to capitalise on such views and challenge further the laws and
practices which disable people in society.

However, some crucial caveats have to be entered as a warning
against any complacency as we look at the prospects for a more inclusive society for disabled people in the next century. First, there is a
danger in focusing on the potential benefits to many disabled people
of a 'wired society' in which new information technologies give them
a 'level playing field' in communicating and working. The gains may
be real, but we have to avoid falling into the trap of overlooking the
financial and other structural barriers to realising these gains; and also
of over-emphasising IT and under-emphasising real social contact in
promoting inclusion, leaving disabled people in an 'electronic ghetto'.

Second, in looking at the long-term future there is a danger of ignoring the many basic features of the problems faced by disabled people
which need recognition and action and which will *not* be amenable to
technological fixes or design improvements to disability aids. These

fundamentals include the poverty afflicting many disabled people and carers, the isolation that both groups can suffer, the inadequacies of the benefits system and of social service and health service care for many people, and the obstacle course of the built environment. There is a risk that technological innovations which assist disabled people will give rise to a feeling that wider changes to the built environment are somehow 'less urgent' as a result.

Most important, there is the cluster of attitudes pervasive among non-disabled citizens when dealing with disabled people: fear, ignorance, lack of empathy, condescension and frustrating token gestures of support. Knight and Brent provide evidence of 'disabling attitudes'.[17] They find that 24 per cent of their sample of 1000 citizens admitted to feeling 'self-conscious and awkward' in the presence of disabled people, and 13 per cent said that they used to feel this way. 43 per cent of respondents also disagreed that a wheelchair user could do their work as well as anyone else: 30 per cent of professionals and 73 per cent of manual workers felt this way about wheelchair users' capabilities. We are still far from an 'inclusive' frame of mind about disabled people's potential and rights as members of 'mainstream' society.

There is also evidence that underlines the extent to which disabled people can be isolated from non-disabled people. According to a 1998 NOP poll a majority (55 per cent) of the public believe that disabled people face social exclusion.[18] This poll found that 53 per cent said that they had *no regular contact* with disabled people. Knight and Brent's 1999 survey of a quota sample of 1000 people indicates that 37 per cent have a close friend or family member with a disability, and 8 per cent have a disabled person living with them; 14 per cent say they have a disabled work colleague. But 41 per cent say that they have no such contact. (This may overstate the situation – government polls suggest that only around one-fifth of the population have no contact; the explanation could lie in the fact that many people covered by official definitions of disability would not describe themselves as disabled, or that many non-disabled people do not recognise the existence of an impairment affecting people they know.) Such results suggest that while many citizens are in regular contact with someone with a disability, a substantial minority are unaware of the challenges that disabled people face, leaving much work to do to educate the public and challenge prejudice.

Leonard Cheshire's survey of opinion formers carried out in summer 1999 points to the importance of routine contact between disabled and non-disabled people.[19] Seventy-seven per cent of respondents felt that disabled people faced social exclusion, and a large majority backed integration of disabled children and adults into the mainstream education system. Respondents reported that a major factor in changing 'excluding' and ill-informed perceptions of disabled citizens' rights, problems and potential was close contact with disabled people. Respondents also favoured measures to ensure that more disabled people gained senior positions in leading organisations and a higher and more positive profile in the media. However, a sign of how far we have to go in achieving greater inclusion of this kind was provided by the survey: not one of the 105 senior people surveyed, drawn from business, media, education, the Civil Service, trade unions and charities, was a disabled person.

Models of disability

Understanding how change might be effected requires understanding of how people perceive disability, and what kinds of exclusion are faced by people with differing impairments. This leads us to consider the different 'models of disability' that have underpinned policy debates in recent decades. This subject is highly complex and has generated a large literature: this is not the place to review the issues in detail. But it is important to outline the debate, since it has significant implications for approaches to twenty-first century social inclusion for disabled people.

The approach of policy-makers, and also of the public, to the problems faced by people with disabilities has traditionally been based on a 'medical model' of disability. This is a way of describing attitudes and analyses which focus on the physical impairments experienced and the adverse effects on 'normal' life which result. Elaborate systems of definition have been built up using medical models, primarily for the purpose of counting disabled people using welfare policies and services. And versions of the medical model are invoked by policy-makers and disability campaigners alike for the assessment of entitlement to benefits.

But reliance on a medical perspective has been vociferously criticised for decades by disability campaigners, who support a 'social model' of disability. This model, which like the medical one has many variants in a wide spectrum of approaches, draws a crucial distinction between 'disability' and 'impairment'. The former is seen as a *social condition*: 'externally imposed disadvantage and social restriction';[20] 'impairment' refers to a medical condition that can become the focus of systematic social exclusion – which is what we should really be referring to when we talk about 'disability'. On this analysis, the medical definition distorts the reality that disability is about dynamic relationships between people and social systems, and is not a static concept.

The social model's perspective also emphasises the dangers of exclusion, prejudice and devaluation of rights that lurk in the medical model, which, as many disability analysts emphasise, is essentially an *individualist* one. The medical model focuses on an individual's impairments and fails to highlight the extent to which these are converted into 'disability' by wider social and environmental factors. The social model stresses by contrast the ways in which the barriers which exclude disabled people from full participation in society are the result of the way the social and built environments are 'constructed'. The problem lies not in the physical impairment but in the way in which institutions and policies fail to meet the needs of people with impairments.

The social model is a powerful critique of the medical view of disability. It switches our perspective from impairments to environments and attitudes. In a sense it parallels the movement, in campaigns over many decades for sexual and racial equality, to reject 'essentialist' explanations for inequality which claimed that women or black people were 'by nature' unsuited to certain jobs or opportunities. It also draws attention to the difficulties involved in using the medical model to define 'disabled people' and count them in a given population: any number we come up with depends on the definition we adopt, and does not reflect the existence of a group of people with some common set of fixed attributes. As Oliver and Barnes put it, 'there is no fixed number of disabled people; disability is dependent on the environments in which impaired people are placed'.[21]

This perspective on disability has its critics, however, within and without the world of disability campaigners: in its strongest form, claiming that nearly all disability is socially constructed and amenable to action, it can seem 'unrealistic'. Plainly, some impairments in some settings *do* 'disable' to a severe degree, constraining what jobs can be done or what skills can be developed. Recognising this need not imply any acceptance of unfair or readily alterable 'disabling' limitations imposed by the environment and by the attitudes of the non-disabled. In some forms too, the social model argument can seem overly 'confrontational', pitting disabled people against a malign environment and placing all the responsibility for change on others.

But despite these qualifications, the social model has huge merits as a way of thinking about disability and inclusion. It is a tool for constructive confrontation of society with its misconceptions about what counts as 'disability'. It draws attention to the immense scope that exists *to prevent or minimise* the disabling obstacles faced by people with impairments, almost regardless of their severity. And most important, in its emphasis on the social and physical environment, it can help overcome the stark 'them-us' distinction inherent in the medical model. It underlines the bonds between people with impairments and those without, by focusing on the disabling effects of particular environments and 'excluding' attitudes. An alternative perspective, drawing on the social model's critique of the medical approach, is the interactionist one – focusing on how particular impairments interact with particular environments.[22] This promises to be a way of looking at problems which can bring together the useful aspects of the medical model's focus on the individual and the social model's crucial focus on disabling barriers in the environment.

Towards a 'mutual model' of disability?

What might the future be for such perspectives based on the insights of the social model of disability? We suggest that campaigning organisations could make more use of them as a tool for promoting greater understanding and inclusion by focusing on a large and still underexplored common ground between disabled people and the (currently) non-disabled. Key aspects of this perspective are summarised below:

- 'The disabled' do not constitute a monolithic social group: whether we use variants of either the medical model or the social model in defining disability, there is a *spectrum of impairment*. It runs from severe long-term constraints on mobility or communication or learning to conditions which have relatively minor impacts on employment chances and ease of negotiating the built and social environments (for example, some skin conditions). The stereotypical image of incapacitated people isolated in special 'homes' is wrong: of over 6 million disabled adults only some 0.4 million live in residential homes or hospitals and so on – the rest are largely householders.[23] Similarly, the image of a wheelchair user as a symbol of disability in much official literature is misleading: it is a minority of disabled people who use wheelchairs – around 5 per cent. Impairment and related 'disability' are *present throughout society*, although not always visible or acknowledged, and the numbers of people affected directly by disability-related exclusion are huge – at least 12 million (disabled people plus carers). And this is not to mention the many family members, friends and colleagues affected indirectly.

- Social exclusion is also not a simple category: it is a complex process of denial or loss of opportunities and social connections. Not all disabled people suffer the same degree or type of exclusion, and many experiences of exclusion are shared with others who are not disabled. This means that measures for greater inclusion of disabled people could assist other excluded people or groups.

- Disability in some form is not the *fate* of a restricted minority, it is a *development* faced by many millions at some point in their lives as a result of impairment, and experience of the full force of the socially constructed disadvantages of disabled people is shared by millions of non-disabled carers. As Kevin Carey has noted, 'It Could Be You' is a message with increasing purchase on public awareness as the population ages and experience of disabling barriers rises.[24]

- This is underlined by the fact that the majority of disabled people become disabled during adult life: 70 per cent of economically active disabled people became disabled while in work.

- *Demographic change* is therefore central to considering the future of policy on disability. The incidence of impairment and long-term illness, and threats to independent living as a result, rise with age. Only 11 per cent of those aged 20 to 29 have a current long-term disability or health problem compared with 30 per cent of those aged 50 to 59.[25] Those experiencing a major form of impairment in youth are in a small minority: 'disability' is closely linked to the ageing process. Given the certainty of the overall 'greying' of society over the coming decades, and in particular as a result of the growth in numbers of the over-80s, experience of some form of significant long-term impairment and of the 'disabling' impact of caring will become increasingly *shared* among all social groups and could become much more salient politically as a result.

- This means that the market for products designed for 'disabled users' is far from a minority niche, as is often assumed: it is a mass market and designs for disability can be seen as *design for universal access*.[26]

- Environmental pressures, demographic change and the demand for new housing over the next ten to fifteen years could also highlight the power of the social model in other ways. A possibility, already present in the concept of the 'lifetime home' (see chapter 3), is that existing forms of 'design for life' are potentially or actually disabling for everyone, and that proper attention to disability access in housing, transport and urban design is actually of benefit to *all* rather than an expensive 'add-on' to 'normal' design.

What these observations point to is an under-explored agenda for mutualism in our understanding of disability and for highlighting shared agendas and the continuum between 'the disabled' and 'the non-disabled'. The currently non-disabled have an interest in the inclusion of disabled people, because impairment can affect *anyone*, and because the resulting 'disability' impacts not only on those with impairments but also on their 'non-disabled' families, friends and relations.

Redesigning workplaces, services and infrastructures is thus not a minority concern but rather a mutual aid project that has inclusive potential for the non-disabled as well as immediate inclusive effect for those disadvantaged by disabling barriers in workplaces and other environments.

If this 'mutual model' for underpinning policy on disability were to be developed, then debates over the exclusion of people with disabilities could change in coming decades. The need will not go away for confrontational debate, strong campaigning against discrimination, and anger, any more than it has in relation to race relations and equality for women. But, as with these areas of equal rights, there is much progress in terms of legislation and changing attitudes on which to build new alliances with other social justice campaigns and to make new partnerships for change with the 'non-disabled' world.

Developments in work, learning, citizenship and the design of the built environment could increase social inclusion for people with disabilities, and campaigning on the basis of the social model and the framework of rights established in the DDA could emphasise the *mutual benefits* to be gained by disabled and non-disabled people alike from this.

In the following chapters we consider some key social developments and their possible impact on the prospects for greater inclusion of disabled people in society and the economy.

1. Work and learning

1.1 Introduction

Powerful forces are transforming the worlds of employment and education and promoting much greater integration between our thinking about work and learning. There is a strong consensus that more 'flexible' forms of work will dominate future labour markets, and that demand for labour will be strongest in fields which call for high levels of adaptability, capacity for learning, information and communication skills, and ability to work well in teams and across functional and sectoral boundaries.

Learning and workplaces will be profoundly affected by the various forces which make up the process we term 'globalisation'. In particular, major change will flow from the advances of information and communication technologies and the growth of sectors in the 'knowledge-intensive' services – the 'weightless' or 'thin air' economy which most new future employment and wealth creation could come from.[27] The 'knowledge economy' of the next century will place a premium on high quality education and capacities of individuals and organisations to carry on learning throughout their lifetimes. These developments pose major challenges to policy on disability: they also open up immense potential for tackling the barriers affecting disabled people.

1.2 Work and inclusion

Work is fundamental to modern notions of social inclusion. It is, for better or worse, a key means of self-definition and establishing the respect of one's peers, and it is the main source of a level of income that underpins a sense of inclusion. Being in paid work has become the badge of 'social inclusion' *par excellence* in the world-view and welfare policies of the New Labour government.

This chapter considers the opportunities and potential problems ahead from likely changes in the world of work. (A more detailed review of some recent research is provided in appendix 1.) It focuses on ways in which a new emphasis on 'work' or 'livelihood' rather than on 'employment' from policy-makers could benefit those facing disadvantage and prejudice. It highlights one potential route to greater inclusion through work, the idea of the 'employee mutual'. It also considers the issue of corporate social responsibility and disability: do employers live up to their responsibilities to promote equal rights and inclusion?

How has the world of work changed? Over the last twenty years the labour market has seen some movement away from full-time to part-time work, leading to an expectation among forecasters amounting to an orthodoxy that work patterns will become more volatile and 'flexible' – with most new jobs created as part-time, temporary or self-employed roles. Part-timers account for around 25 per cent of the workforce, up from a fifth in 1980, with part-time work dominated by women (82 per cent of part-timers). Self-employment grew from 1.9 million people in 1979 to 3.3 million by 1997. The workforce has changed substantially in recent years, with a big rise in women in work, and a steady decline in the activity of men aged 55 or over.

These changes have been accompanied by a large-scale adoption of new information and communications technology. This has allowed greater flexibility in work location in many sectors, in principle allowing people to operate more of the time as 'teleworkers'. Manufacturing employment has declined sharply and most new jobs are created in the service economy. Working hours for many have risen, and there are now 1.2 million people with two jobs, nearly twice the number in 1984 – and some two-thirds of them are women. Flexibility in work has also meant increases in evening, shift and weekend working. There is also evidence of a rise in the pressure of deadlines and demands as work has *intensified* in many workplaces, raising concerns over the impact of the emerging world of work on family life and well-being for many people.[28]

This intensification seems to be linked to changes in the organisation of work. As industrial production and competition spread round the globe, and as new technologies sharpen competitive forces, so companies have reorganised, shed labour, and been placed under greater pressures for maximising returns to shareholders. In some sectors the rise of developing countries as production centres has made it possible to close down UK capacity, and this might happen to a greater extent in future, in service sectors as well as in manufacturing. In the public sector too, spending constraints stemming from the move towards a lower-tax economy have increased pressures for greater efficiencies at work.

All these factors have raised the stakes for remaining employees and have made it harder for those who lose their jobs to get back into work at their previous level. While insecurity does not seem to have risen much over the last decade in terms of job tenure – indeed, for many women, average length of time in jobs has risen – there is little doubt that feelings of insecurity have persisted for many people since the recession of 1990–93 despite the economic recovery. Changes at work have continued to keep many people feeling insecure, if not about losing their jobs then about their long term prospects and their conditions of work. They have also eroded the old 'psychological contract' of loyalty between employers and staff and make it hard for many managers to maintain 'a credible commitment to the health and security' of employees, and also to the demands of equal opportunities legislation and corporate aspirations to workplace equality.[29]

The rising pressures of being in work have been matched by growing problems for those out of a job: the chances of becoming long-term unemployed or inactive after losing a job have risen. The chances of moving from unemployment to inactivity more than doubled between 1977 and 1995. One-quarter of those gaining jobs after unemployment are back on the register within three months, having typically taken a cut in pay relative to previous pay when in work. In short, while many new opportunities and jobs have been created in the last ten to fifteen years of labour market change, with many high rewards and improvements in workplace conditions, so the risks of exclusion and feelings of insecurity also seem to have risen.

So much for the general background. What about the access of disabled people to work? The basic facts about disability and employment are that disabled people are more likely than the non-disabled to be unemployed, long-term unemployed, in low-paid and low-skilled jobs, and that many who become disabled while in work may subsequently have to leave employment for want of appropriate job changes. Many disabled people not in paid work would like to be, and many who leave jobs would like to stay in them. Many also face prejudice and lack of awareness of their needs and potential contribution from employers. Key statistics about disability and employment are summed up in Figure 1 below.

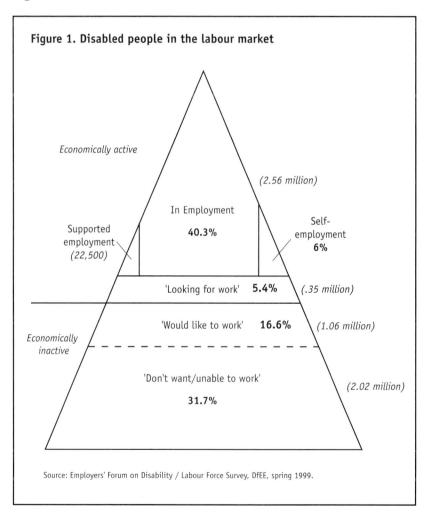

Figure 1. Disabled people in the labour market

Economically active

(2.56 million)

In Employment

40.3%

Supported employment (22,500)

Self-employment **6%**

'Looking for work' **5.4%** (.35 million)

'Would like to work' **16.6%** (1.06 million)

Economically inactive

'Don't want/unable to work' (2.02 million)

31.7%

Source: Employers' Forum on Disability / Labour Force Survey, DfEE, spring 1999.

So a widely accepted vision of the future of work, avoiding exaggerated claims for the impact of new technologies, might be as follows:

- The global spread of industrial production and competition, boosted by the development of new information and communication technologies, will continue to put pressure on jobs and traditional work arrangements as employers face more intense competition on cost, quality and flexibility of service.
- Many millions of people in work are and by 2010 still will be in full-time posts, but as a proportion of total employment full-time permanent positions will be falling in importance for the next ten to fifteen years.
- There are increasing returns to qualifications, specialised technical skills, IT skills, and high level knowledge throughout the economy: a large gap has opened up in pay and prospects between the higher-skilled and those with few or no qualifications.
- Average job tenure is likely to continue to decline gradually in many sectors for men, and may begin to decline also for women.
- Redundancy programmes, driven by scope for reducing labour through use of new technology, outsourcing and organisational change (such as mergers and acquisitions) will continue to be a feature of life almost regardless of the overall state of the economy, as competition sharpens in an internationalised trading system.
- The risks from episodes of unemployment of either staying jobless or having to return to work at a lower level of pay and prospects have apparently gone up, and it remains to be seen how successful over the long run new strategies for welfare-to-work transition such as the New Deal turn out to be.
- part-time work, temporary jobs and self-employment have all grown as a proportion of overall employment and are likely to continue doing so.
- Hours of work are becoming more flexible in many jobs and have increased for many in managerial and professional jobs, and also probably for many in lower-level occupations; these trends seem likely to continue.
- Employment on contracts through intermediary recruitment agencies has increased as a proportion of those in temporary work.

- Self-employment and micro-enterprises are expected by many fore-casters to be the main engines of growth in employment in the new century.

What might this mean for the prospects of disabled people? Some suggestions are made below about the potential benefits and problems for disabled people which the trends in labour markets could bring.

There will be a premium on high levels of adaptability, knowledge, information and communication skills in the growth sectors of the next ten to fifteen years (creative industries, IT, training and education of all kinds, personal care services, management services, financial services, and so on). Potentially this places many disabled people – especially those with learning difficulties – at an even *greater* disadvantage, given that on average their skill and qualification levels are lower than among non-disabled people, and that many lack opportunities to make extensive social contacts in an age that increasingly values networking and communication skills in work. This implies that raising access to high quality education and training and to wider networks of support will be a key element of campaigns for equal rights and opportunities for disabled people in future.

The extent to which opportunities in the labour market are now polar-ising between people with in-demand skills and those without, or are thought to lack them, will not necessarily hurt all disabled people. As one speaker put it at the symposium, 'the disabled elite' of campaign-ers, researchers, policy-makers and others will not find their position much affected; but the emerging trends could make life chances *worse* for the more vulnerable of disabled people.

Can we identify any factors which could improve the outlook? There is also likely to be an increase in the exposure of many *non-disabled* as well as disabled people to redundancy, to downward mobility, to volatile employment conditions, to possibly damaging intensification of work, and to the need to rethink their aims and prospects funda-mentally, and to the need to enter part-time, temporary or self-employed work. All this potentially opens up a large common ground with many disabled people. It could be the basis for communication of shared concerns, and campaigning in partnerships, across the disabled/non-disabled divide.

Conceivably, in the search for highly adaptable and resilient workers in sectors suffering from skill shortages (especially the IT sector and education), many organisations could find that many disabled people, especially given access to well-designed and appropriate IT systems and given management commitment to workplace equality, could be highly desirable recruits on the basis of their skills and also their experience in overcoming pervasive obstacles.[30] Similar arguments can be made about others facing barriers to 'inclusion' – such as single mothers on low incomes. This points to scope for broadly-based alliances of campaigners to change employers' perceptions of disadvantaged groups across the board, not simply in relation to disability.

This is potentially the case in a broad and ill-defined 'sector' which many forecasters expect to become significant as a source of work, especially in self-employment – personal mentoring, coaching and facilitation. In education and staff development, there is a growing recognition of the need for improved 'emotional intelligence' and for mentoring for people at many levels, not only among those in work but also for those on welfare-to-work options and those young people who are alienated from education and training programmes. As yet mentoring is an idea widely acclaimed and piloted, and seen as a key element in a 'learning society' (see section 1.3) but which has yet to develop systems for training and accreditation. Conceivably this is a field which is 'disability-blind' also, in which disabled people could find much work.

Many jobs will be increasingly dependent on the use of advanced information and communications technologies. There is great scope here for more job openings for disabled people, and for much more retention of newly-disabled people in work, since many advances in information technology (see chapter 3) can assist them to communicate on equal 'virtual' terms with the non-disabled. Against this, there is the widely noted increase in the pace of work and information throughput in many workplaces, which could disadvantage severely disabled people (and many others, non-disabled as well as disabled) who need to be able to work at a variable pace. And there is also the risk that new technological aids for disabled people will be used to 'fix the person' rather than to 'fix the place', leaving disabling features of the wider workplace environment unaltered.

But the possibilities for 'fixing the place' in advance could be expanded in future. Potentially, the likelihood that many new jobs will be created in brand new enterprises of different kinds opens up the possibility for *much more attention from the outset* to the scope for 'designing in' access for disabled workers in terms of physical access and the design of workplaces and jobs.

The increase in self-employment could benefit disabled people since, according to the LFS[31] they are slightly more likely to be self-employed than non-disabled people. But this should be set against the consideration that self-employed people are likely to be under greater pressure to work longer hours, which may not be an option for many disabled people.

There are substantial psychological barriers to overcome for many disabled people seeking employment. These include a sense of underestimation of their own potential, and there may be a role for mentors for many disabled people who have been economically inactive in order to enhance self-esteem. But there is equally room for people to use their experience of disability in a positive way to contribute by using skills of empathy and problem solving which they may have had to develop. In some employment settings disability may itself be a qualification and/or an asset for the job – this is especially true in the field of care-work or social policy research on disability.

LFS data show that many disabled people want work but are not immediately ready for jobs, and many are unlikely to gain mainstream employment in the face of pervasive prejudice and lack of awareness of disability, the DDA and the scope for integration. Moreover, the future of welfare provision seems to be based on the principle of 'no benefit without willingness to work where possible': one corollary must be, if such a stance is to be politically viable over the long run in the conditions of globalisation and flexibility, that *the state and its partners will generate work which pays a decent wage when and where the market cannot.* (See also chapter 2 on welfare issues.)

Accordingly there will be a continuing need for the development of intermediate labour markets (ILMs), with the state as employer or (more likely) funding source of last resort. ILMs will be run through many intermediate voluntary or mutual organisations acting as employers, providing socially desirable services and chances for work experience and training outside a market framework. Providers of such services and ILM systems include major voluntary bodies such as the regeneration body Groundwork and many charities, including disability organisations. Areas in which such systems could develop specialisms include education, training, mentoring, community development and community information services, and personal services of various kinds.

A related area for continuing innovation is the design and development of intermediate employment models, especially those opening up opportunities for people with learning disabilities or impairments which put them at a severe disadvantage in gaining mainstream jobs. These models include supported employment, for which there seems to be potential demand for a big expansion of the existing 22,000,[32] and therapeutic sheltered employment for those with mental health problems. But it must be noted that neither of these is as desirable as 'non-segregated' work and inclusion in mainstream work settings. government policy recognises this: but it has yet to show how disabled people displaced from supported employment (as at Remploy in 1999) will find suitable jobs in the mainstream.

ILM development could be stimulated by outsourcing of work by firms, public authorities and other bodies as part of socially and environmentally responsive purchasing strategies – such as the 'Best Value' system being adopted by local authorities in the UK. But this depends on strong and clear guidance to local authorities and other public agencies from central government and rigorous monitoring of the implementation of Best Value.

It is likely that welfare-to-work programmes will be a substantial feature of employment policy for the next ten to fifteen years, especially since over the next few years we are likely to experience further shake-outs of jobs across the board as a result of recession and global economic turbulence. As this happens, and as perhaps more people reject the stressful long-hours culture of many organisations, there is likely to be increasing emphasis on 'work' as opposed to 'employment' as a yardstick for social inclusion. This will mean more interest in informal livelihood (volunteer work, caring, LETS – Local Exchange and Trading Schemes, systems for local swapping of services based on a 'currency' of tokens or credits – and varieties of mutual aid schemes), probably manifested in new ways of combining benefits with socially valuable work, or of mixing benefits and paid work.[33]

A central feature of such programmes is likely to be extensive work experience, whether in mainstream jobs or ILMs, and for disabled people and non-disabled alike these offer the opportunity for far more contact than might otherwise ensue in the world of work. The development of more diverse New Deal programmes, which do not recognise a division between disabled people and the non-disabled, could emerge if experience of welfare-to-work in some form becomes much more common in the new century because of the volatility of globalising markets and the impact of technology and changing demands on workers.

The employee mutual – a way ahead?

A possible development in the labour market which reflects the known and emerging trends and which could be a powerful force for integration and enhanced opportunities for work (as opposed to 'jobs') for disabled people is proposed in Charles Leadbeater and Stephen Martin's book *The Employee Mutual: Combining flexibility with security in the new world of work*.[34]

The idea of the employee mutual (EM) is of a new form of labour market body, a blend of recruitment agency, training provider, trade union, mutual aid association and co-operative enterprise. It would match the need of modern organisations for flexible labour with the need of workers for a measure of security and for sharing costs and risks in paying for training, childcare, working aids and so on.

The EM idea is now being considered seriously by a range of organisations as a scheme which should be piloted. The book suggests that by 2010 a national programme of pilots could have created a new set of organisations and standards which would valuably complement existing institutions. The EM would:

- be a membership organisation that would be open to the unemployed, self-employed, employed and employers;
- integrate people with impairments and without;
- help people find work, develop skills, manage their working lives;

- help employers fill vacancies and bring together workers and organisations to meet shared needs for childcare, training and other needs – which could include shared costs for investment in improved disability access and new IT systems;
- help overcome benefit and poverty traps by offering a flexible means of administering benefits and welfare-to-work programmes;
- offer networking and a 'club' ethos that would bring together employed and unemployed people, expanding the range of social contacts for isolated people;
- be funded by membership subscriptions, employers, the State, local government and through the provision of services in the market.

The EM concept could have much to offer many disabled people. It would combine a supportive and fully integrated environment for them to find work of different kinds with plentiful access to support services. A vital feature for many isolated people with low social confidence and skills would be the promotion of social contacts of a richly varied kind, from which further leads for employment and self-employed assignments might flow.

The employee mutual organisation would also offer start-up business support and training support services of the kind offered by TECs and Business Links, albeit patchily and with limited impact to date on disabled people; but it would have the advantage of adding a membership system and associated services and benefits. It could also be a framework within which carers could develop skills, learn from each other, support each other, lobby for resources, gain respite breaks and share tasks (why not team-caring?). Such developments might well occur on a large scale as the flexible labour market generates more insecurity and dissatisfaction and as the proportion of potentially vulnerable people in temporary and self-employed work grows.

The mutual is no panacea: it will not be *the* answer to lack of work opportunities. But it illustrates the need to think radically about ways of opening up work to more people who want it. Regardless of the take-up or not of the idea, the fact is that such innovations, and a more flexible approach to combining work with welfare and to ILM development, will be essential in the job markets of the future. If we believe that work is the touchstone of inclusion, then we cannot take a fatalistic view of the impact of globalisation, new technology and work reorganisation on jobs. Many disabled people will remain excluded, and many will become still more vulnerable, as these changes continue. But the new 'thin air economy' and the growth of new services will generate more opportunities too for disabled people. Many will need support in taking them, in the form of new training, improved aids to reduce the effect of impairments, and access to more flexible packages of assistance in moving from welfare dependency to livelihood.

For those who remain excluded from work, two key steps will be necessary. First, strong enforcement of disability rights via the DDA, so that discrimination is tackled. Second, action to back up the government's recognition that some will not get paid work and need decent levels of support through the benefits system. This point is taken up in chapter 2.

Employers' perceptions and corporate responsibility
In transforming the labour market to better suit the needs of disabled people it is widely seen as essential to argue the 'business case' for change, not simply the rights-based case.[35] It is argued that only when business can see real benefit (financial or in other tangible terms) from a more inclusive approach to disability will there be a substantial shift in attitudes and workplace practice, dominated as these are by ignorance, fear, inertia and a view that disabled people are somehow 'naturally' excluded.

Expert observers interviewed in the preparation of this report felt that the business case for taking disability seriously has not been making as much progress as similar appeals to enlightened self-interest in relation to employing women and people from ethnic minorities. In a recent review of an international gathering of executives from major firms to discuss corporate social responsibility, David Grayson noted with regret the lack of interest in disability issues, which appeared to be seen as a 'Cinderella' subject. Grayson has also pointed to the low profile of disability rights by comparison with other equality issues, environmental responsibility and community investment in the strategies of even the major firms which have taken corporate social responsibility most seriously.[36]

However, the advocacy and research carried out in recent years by the Employers' Forum on Disability (EFD) shows how effective communication tools can be designed and delivered for overcoming ignorance and distorted perceptions of the issues around employment and disability. The EFD has focused especially on building up a hard-nosed commercial case for taking disability rights seriously as well as appealing to employers' sense of social responsibility. Its report on the business case notes that by excluding disabled people from its staffing, marketing and product/service design, business is missing out on a great chance to improve long-term profitability and is ignoring a large and growing market of disabled people who represent valuable skills and consumer demand, if only these were recognised as they should be.[37]

A clear trend for the next ten years is the growth of pressure on businesses to become far more accountable in relation to their impact on the well-being of society and the environment. This process is driven by a number of factors:

- the rise of competition in many markets on a global scale, which has reduced the competitive edge from product quality and price and heightened the differential advantages to be gained from maximising *public trust and approval*, and from avoidance of bad publicity, regulatory conflicts and clashes with powerful and well-respected non-profit organisations (as in the case of Shell versus Greenpeace);
- the rise of awareness of environmental and social degradation in developing countries and increasing pressure on multinationals to apply high standards in environmental and social care to their developing world operations;
- rising public concern in the West over environmental damage and risks from innovations (as in the case of genetic modification of food);
- intensifying scrutiny of business by the media and campaigning NGOs, assisted enormously by the rise of global electronic communications, and developing greater sophistication as the Internet develops;
- the likely growth of innovative forms of workplace democracy and consultation with corporate 'stakeholders', exposing more employ-

ers to advocacy of measures to tackle discrimination and low representation of disadvantaged groups in the workforce;

- the development by organisations such as Business in the Community of a coherent and increasingly well-documented argument that corporate community involvement (CCI) is likely to deliver tangible and intangible benefits for companies, ranging from improved financial performance to better retention and recruitment of high-quality staff and better relations with local communities and the public at large;

- the prospect of continuing growth in corporate membership of the Employers' Forum on Disability and increasing influence for EFD's articulation of the business case for proactive initiatives on a fair deal for disabled people in employment;

- the likelihood of a higher profile for government statements of the need for social responsibility in business in general, and of the need for employers to work constructively with the new Disability Rights Commission in implementing the DDA and pursuing good practice as advocated by the EFD and other campaigning and advisory organisations.

These trends will in all probability continue and intensify in many cases over the next ten to fifteen years. The result is likely to be:

- an increasing number of companies producing regular social and environment impact reports alongside or as part of the annual report;

- growing professionalism among leading firms in devising and managing corporate citizenship policies and in working in partnership with campaign organisations and with public initiatives such as the New Deal;

- more non-profit organisations acting as 'quasi-regulators', researching and verifying corporate statements and publicising successes and shortcomings, and hired by firms precisely because of the high level of public trust they tend to command;

- rising expectations among new recruits and existing employees of standards of corporate social and environmental responsibility.

These developments should open up new opportunities to promote the integration of disability awareness and proper attention to legal and wider social responsibilities in relation to disabled people's prospects. More ambitiously, we can speculate on what might happen as improved measures of corporate impact are developed. A development which would fit with the emerging trends noted above and with the pervasive desire among policy-makers to be 'business-friendly' in a globalising environment for regulation would be efforts to link achievement of key social and environmental standards above the legal requirement with corporation tax breaks or tax holidays, providing an incentive for high levels of performance as an investor in people, environment and community, and for internalisation of social and environmental costs currently off-loaded on to society at large.[38] Obviously excellence in disability access and implementation of equality policy would be part of any such scheme – which, it must be acknowledged, would be complex to design and monitor.

More practically, there is obviously huge scope for improving employers' awareness of the needs of disabled people and their own need to work with the DDA and the DRC, for streamlining employers' contact points in government and agencies dealing with disability, and for improving the quality of information and expert advice available to firms about the innovative charities and disability training providers with which business will wish to work.[39] Initiatives such as Leonard Cheshire's 'Workability' programme to assist disabled people into work by giving better access to IT skills and services in partnership with employers point to the large scope available for more and better partnerships between employers, disability organisations and other bodies.

As companies adopt new technologies and restructure offices at great expense to capture new productivity gains, follow fashion and improve conditions – likely to be a continuing feature of organisational life for the next ten to fifteen years – there will be opportunities for policy-makers, employer-led bodies such as EFD and the CBI, and disability campaign bodies to point out the many openings this provides for designing in disability access from the outset. Moreover, many adjustments may be of *wider benefit to non-disabled staff and visitors*. There will also be scope for researching and highlighting the real costs of providing full disability access (physical and virtual) and providing aids and adjustments, which in many cases are likely to be low by comparison with the costs of developing new offices, Intranets and new Internet systems, and so on.

This is underlined by recent research: Meager, Evans et al found that in their survey of 1,500 service providers about disability provision 'cost was not raised as a major issue' either by those providing access improvements or those failing to make any.[40] Moreover, Meager et al found that 85 per cent of disabled people in their sample said they did not need adaptations to get into a building or use its facilities, and fewer than 15 per cent said they needed some form of special aids to work.[41] In the future context of a flexible and increasingly IT-intensive work-place, which is regularly overhauled and is going to be highly adaptable to the needs of many disabled people, the probability is that the real cost of providing aids and access improvements is *over-estimated* by many organisations and policy-makers. government figures on DDA compli-ance costs from research based on 40 case studies of employers show that 44 per cent of adjustments to help disabled employees function effectively at work cost between nil and £49, and that just 5 per cent of adjustments cost more than £5,000.

Ways to promote the benefits of excellence in disability access – rewarding organisations which go beyond the demands of legislation and demonstrate commitment to facilitating independence for disabled people – could include:

- use of a stream of Lottery funding to provide part-funding for excel-lent adaptation schemes designed in partnership with disabled users;
- wider promotion of the new Adapt Trust awards for excellent disability access;
- building in compliance with DDA provisions and best practice in access to Best Value purchasing criteria for appropriate public sector contracts – this could be a powerful tool for raising awareness and prompting action by employers who have yet to take disability rights seriously enough;
- aggressive campaigning by business representative organisations such as Employers' Forum on Disability and Business in the Community to raise the performance of member companies

committed to high standards in disability equality policies in the light of the often poor access available at premises of 50 of the largest companies in the UK;[42]

- this should include advocacy of the full integration of disability equality – and that of other forms of equal opportunities and social and environmental responsibility – in the mainstream decision making and strategies of employers; the inclusion of disability as an issue in the 'community affairs' function of many big companies should be seen as a *transitional* phase in raising awareness, not as the end of the process;
- regular reinforcement through clear and prominent statements by Cabinet Ministers of the importance of social inclusion for disabled people and of the rights-based and business cases for full compliance with the DDA and good practice as promoted by bodies such as EFD.

Will such measures be enough? The evidence from the development of equal rights programmes is that while voluntarism and codes of conduct are vital in helping change cultures of discrimination, they are *not* sufficient. The firm enforcement of the DDA and the extension of 'naming and shaming' of poorly performing employers by government and campaigners is also necessary. Women's rights and equal rights for ethnic minorities have been promoted by use of the law as well as campaigns to change hearts and minds. Ageism in the workplace, which is evidently widespread, is likely to be tackled effectively only when exhortation and good practice guides are backed by legislation to restrict age discrimination in work. Disability discrimination will be combated by a combination of law and culture-changing strategies, and these must go hand in hand.

1.3 Learning and inclusion

The quality of our experience of compulsory education and of the learning opportunities we have is now recognised as fundamental to future prospects in work, to quality of life and to a fully 'included' life as a citizen. For many disabled people exclusion is embedded in their lives at an early stage through poor education. Progress towards a high standard of educational experience for all is vital for disabled people's chances of social inclusion and equality. This section looks at the development of a 'learning society' and what opportunities and potential problems this throws up for disabled people. The section also looks at the learning that needs to be done by the *non-disabled population* before we can consider that disabled people have been properly 'included' as equal citizens. An issue highlighted is the rise of the 'learning state' – the growing emphasis of policy-makers and service providers on evaluation and new indicators.

Towards a 'learning society'?
The government has made the improvement of national education systems a key part of its long-term strategy to overcome social exclusion and raise economic performance.[43] Initiatives are being developed on several fronts, all within a general vision of a 'learning society' in which early educational experience will be a solid foundation for thriving in work and social relationships, followed by experience of a flexible post-school system of further and higher education which will be open to many more people than ever before, in order to meet the demand for 'lifelong learning' in a high-tech, knowledge-intensive economy, and also to stimulate habits of continuous self-improvement. Initiatives which we can expect to continue to develop over the next decade include:

- the development of new performance targets for schools and other centres of learning, and of new forms of school management;
- more diversity of management and focus for schools (such as technology schools) within a national framework of standards and targets;
- new emphasis on civic and moral education;
- major emphasis on new information and communication technologies as learning tools, especially via the planned 'National Grid for Learning', a 'superhighway' network linking schools to the Internet;
- new means of accessing information technology for disabled people (see chapter 2) open up many opportunities for participation in networked learning and use of Internet resources;

- radical rethinking of the training, development and role of teachers in primary and secondary schools, with more emphasis on teachers as facilitators and mentors, with more jobs opening up for a new breed of teacher-assistants in guiding and supervising pupils, and with far more interchange between the teaching world and other occupations, for example, in the form of secondments;
- pressure for an opening up of the crowded and rigid National Curriculum, with more scope for team working, diverse forms of study and work experience, and less individualised achievement standards, developments which would benefit many disabled people, but not only them;[44]
- development of new forms of financial support for learning, for example, via Individual Learning Accounts;
- a move towards promoting opportunities for learning in many settings beyond schools, colleges and universities, making use of new IT tools, community consultation processes (see chapters 2 and 3) and connections between educational institutions and other bodies (see Figure 2 opposite);[45]
- the creation of a University for Industry;
- a move, already seen in the new National Framework for Study Support, towards multiple use of existing settings for learning which are presently 'exclusive' – opening up schools far more for evening, weekend and holiday use as learning centres for adults, or even linking them with new services in preventive healthcare (such as the proposed 'healthy living centres') and welfare (the new 'One' gateway service for claimants) to form *neighbourhood learning centres* or hubs of community learning networks;[46]
- new outlets and multi-agency strategies for lifelong learning – such as the 'learning shop' in Norwich for drop-in adult education services and the 'networks of learning' approach developed in Birmingham;[47]
- initiatives to promote new *communal* learning – for example, about the possible futures for one's neighbourhood or city or industry, or about the policy options in a controversial field such as waste disposal or new house-building: these include citizens' juries, visioning exercises, community planning consultations, and so on

---

Figure 2. Settings for learning

Obvious: pre-school groups; nurseries; schools; colleges; universities; adult education centres; homes; libraries; television

Less obvious: businesses; community centres; arts centres; museums and attractions; health centres; post offices; citizens' advice bureaux; cities; towns; villages; Internet; nature reserves; the outdoors; newspapers; bookshops

Surprising: old people's homes; homeless shelters; refuges; prisons; shopping malls; hospitals; churches; trains; stations; football stadia; service stations; restaurants; hotels; cafes; night-clubs; local parks

Source: Cara et al, 1998, *The Learning City in the Learning Age*, Comedia/Demos, London.

– all of which could be refined in many ways by using new interactive media and other techniques for group learning;[48]

- much greater use of work and volunteering experience as a core element of secondary and tertiary education, further breaking down barriers between schools and the wider community, and between types of school and college; a radical possibility over the long term might be the lowering of the school-leaving age to fourteen, with early leavers given individual learning packages in different settings, providing a mixture of core curricular learning, work experience and volunteering.[49] This kind of development is likely to be of great value to disabled students: despite increases in participation in further and higher education, and advances in qualification levels, these results have yet to be translated into better job prospects for many. Better work experience opportunities for disabled students could be a key factor in boosting their employability.

Plainly there are many ways in which such developments could advance the social inclusion of people with disabilities: making learning far less dependent on access to a particular place, opening up high quality learning tools and materials to a much bigger audience via the Internet and National Grid for Learning, and providing scope for more contact between disabled and non-disabled people from an early age and at all ages. The idea of the neighbourhood learning centre, in which specialist provision for disabled students could co-exist with spaces and times for integrated learning, is an attractive one.

But many obstacles stand in the way of the learning society vision:

- some special schools for disabled people may have lower standards and expectations of students than mainstream ones, and can reinforce an 'excluded' image and self-image;
- inadequate physical access for wheelchair users and visually impaired people to many school and college buildings, and to other sites that might become learning centres in future; and poor facilities for people with these and other impairments inside the buildings;
- although most disabled children are already in mainstream schools, disability access is limited and their disadvantage may be exacerbated by the fact that overall quality standards and expectations in many mainstream schools are unacceptable and will take time and money to raise;
- the disadvantage faced by people with learning disabilities will be compounded by advances by the wider population and we will require special efforts from policy-makers and learning system designers to find ways of reducing it;
- integration of disabled people in mainstream schools on its own does not guarantee improved chances in education and later: in a Scope survey of disabled people 53 per cent of respondents felt that they had been treated differently at school. The study also found that 41 per cent felt that teachers in mainstream schools had *underestimated* their ability, as did 43 per cent of those who attended special schools;[50]
- the cost of taking advantage of learning opportunities, especially in higher education and especially for mature students, may be

prohibitive for many, especially for disabled people facing other costs for aids and adaptations in a harsh funding environment; new thinking will be needed on how disadvantaged people generally, and disabled people in particular, can be assisted to afford learning opportunities, via Learning Accounts and other mechanisms;

- the risks of 'information exclusion' noted in chapter 2;
- the risk that new services and facilities will not be designed with universal access in mind – Internet-based services and new settings for learning need to be designed from the outset with disability equality in mind;
- public spending constraints and institutional inertia and lack of disability awareness in the school system – although it should be noted that the Schools Access initiative, designed to improve disability access in mainstream schools, has been allocated £20 million by government for 1999–2000, a significant increase on previous years, and that government has committed itself to a sustained programme for improved school accessibility;
- the fact that education is still not covered by the 1995 DDA's provisions covering access to services (although many establishments may nonetheless have developed good access facilities for disabled people already).

Other issues are raised by the post-school learning environment, in particular in relation to employers. There is concern reported in the research literature that the type of training which many disabled people tend to receive is geared to pre-conceived and stereotypical notions about the kinds of training they need. In effect, rather than adhering to the social model of disability and providing training for disabled people according to the nature of the (changing) labour market, the training offered has tended to have pre-determined 'realistic' limits – which may well grossly underestimate what someone is capable of and wishes to achieve.

There is also concern over the degree to which training providers, TECs, Business Links and other intermediaries between education institutions and employers take account of the needs and potential of the local disabled population and educate employers about their responsibilities and opportunities. All of these concerns over employers' commitment to training and training agencies' co-ordination and coherence in assisting socially excluded people, of course, apply as well to other disadvantaged groups, notably from ethnic minority communities and low-income, low-skill groups generally. Meeting the challenges in this area is not simply a matter of assisting disabled people alone: once again, there is a much wider 'mutualist' agenda here with which disabled people's organisations can work.

The future could be an optimistic one. There is a strong impetus at many levels towards a more flexible education and training system in which the rigid boundaries between sectors, institutions, settings for learning and education providers and the wider community are eroded and productive mixing and matching of people, opportunities and needs can happen. Recent official reports on the future of education and skills development have emphasised the need for much greater customisation of provision – fitting learning establishments to the needs of the individual learner rather than vice versa. For disabled people, such developments hold out the prospect of much improved virtual access to education and training, and new opportunities for learning in many integrated settings and for much more social contact between disabled and non-disabled people at all ages.

The key change in any move towards 'an inclusive future' may be more determination in ensuring that primary and secondary schools are places where disabled and non-disabled pupils mix and learn to understand and accept each other's differences and potential and to respect each other's rights. The Scope survey of schools' access for disabled children concluded that the cost of making 75 per cent of primary schools and 50 per cent of secondary schools accessible, and paying for related training for staff, would be some £310 million, a modest amount in the context of total education spending.[51] As schools seek to become 'community schools' and as a new citizenship curriculum is developed, pressure will grow for disability to be taken more seriously as part of mainstream learning and educational design. The extension of the DDA to cover schools will be increasingly seen as a vital improvement to the law and should be viewed as part of an overall investment in integrated education, which must be the foundation for a more inclusive society in the long term.

The learning state and the learning community

As noted earlier, the attempt is being made to develop more 'holistic' policy in many areas, with greater attention to measuring outcomes and devising indicators of performance which reflect the 'joined-up' nature of many problems, especially in relation to social exclusion. There is a trend towards explicit evaluation of performance in many parts of the public sector and among its partners on the basis of new outcome measures in an effort to improve results and learn from pilot schemes. The state is trying to become a 'learning system', capturing lessons from pilots, past mistakes and successes, and results of local initiatives around the country and abroad.

A key feature of this movement is the development of new indicators at national, regional and local level. This has been stimulated by government audit demands and initiatives such as Local Agenda 21, an action plan for local authorities to pursue sustainable development, and by many critiques of the one-dimensional economic indicators which are used as a guide to progress in quality of life. New attempts to measure quality of life are being explored by central and local government, principally as a result of pressure for better indicators of environmental sustainability and community well-being, and will become more important to policy-making and more visible to the public over the next decade. It will be important for disability organisations to influence such indicator sets as a way of promoting the full integration of the disability agenda into the design and evaluation of 'joined up policies'.

Indicators of community well-being have been developed experimentally on a large scale at local level.[52] This usually involves a major consultative exercise, and can be seen as an aspect of the development of a 'learning community', bringing opportunities for highlighting the needs and contributions of disabled people and carers. Many new forums for mutual learning will develop as policy-makers and service providers seek to raise the performance of services and to avoid the mistakes associated with a top-down and paternalist culture of service delivery to 'clients'. Such community learning initiatives will proliferate as local government seeks new legitimacy (see chapter 2) and new processes to encourage public participation. Again, there is a need and opportunity for disability awareness to be 'designed in' from the outset in many cases, promoting better public knowledge of disability issues.

Educating the non-disabled
Many of the measures discussed above will have the effect of making disability more visible to a wide public, and of bringing non-disabled people into more regular contact with disabled people. These developments could generate a gradual and effective process of learning.

But plainly there will be a great need for further measures of public education and awareness-raising among employers and organisations. Opportunities arising over the period to 2010 include:

● the launch of the DRC and subsequent anniversaries;
● fifth, tenth and fifteenth anniversaries of the DDA;
● implementation of successive phases of the DDA;
● debate over improvements to the DDA and over the impact on disabled people's opportunities of new legislative proposals;
● debate over universal access to the Internet and the National Grid for Learning;
● integration of disability awareness into civic and moral education in the core curriculum;[53]
● integration of contact between disabled and non-disabled people in work experience and volunteering elements of a revised core curriculum;
● pressure for more representation of disabled people in the mass media, with debate stimulated by moves towards wider channel provision on digital TV;
● further promotion of corporate community involvement and employee volunteering could highlight disability issues as key areas still to be addressed adequately by employers;
● debates following the launch of major policy initiatives relevant to disabled people, for example any large-scale piloting of the employee mutual concept (see pages 37–38).

1.4 Conclusions: action for inclusion
Major changes in the worlds of work and learning open up many new opportunities for inclusion of disabled people, but they also present

risks of further exclusion. Innovative policies are needed to seize the opportunities that are emerging and to prevent further disadvantage for many people in the flexible and demanding labour market of the new century.

With the emphasis now placed on participation in work as a touchstone of social inclusion, more efforts need to be made to tackle discrimination in workplaces and in recruitment, through enforcement of the DDA, regular high-profile messages from ministers to employers in all sectors, and strong partnerships between the DRC and employers' bodies such as Business in the Community and the Employers' Forum on Disability. These should emphasise that equal opportunities for disabled people are both a matter of civil rights and also of harnessing business opportunities; and that disability is a mainstream strategic issue, not a marginal element of 'corporate community relations'.

We also need innovation from government and partners in business and the voluntary sector in promoting opportunities that include disadvantaged disabled people and non-disabled people alike in the mainstream of work. This will call for more commitment to promoting disability equality from labour market intermediaries such as TECs and their successors, and experiments in new forms of organisation which fit the nature of the emerging flexible labour market. We have outlined a vision of such an inclusive body, the employee mutual. This should be piloted by a range of partners from the public, private and voluntary sectors to find out its strengths and weaknesses.

Inclusion in work and employability begins with education. A key reform will be the extension of the DDA to cover all educational establishments, in order to boost integration of disabled students in mainstream learning wherever possible. We will also need pre-emptive involvement of disabled people in the design of new institutions and facilities for lifetime learning, such as the National Grid Internet system.

Above all, we need a national debate on how we can achieve real inclusion for all in a changing world of work and education, and the development of a shared strategy for helping people – disabled and non-disabled alike – move from welfare to work and from learning to work. The DRC, EFD and BitC could create a coalition of partners within and outside the disability world involved in implementing the modernisation agenda in work and learning to devise a common vision, identify solutions and press for their implementation.

2. Citizenship

2.1 Introduction

This chapter considers the idea of citizenship, a fundamental element in any sense of 'social inclusion'. The next two decades will see major changes in our understanding of citizenship. Disability rights will be enshrined alongside other rights to equality, and a Bill of Rights might yet become part of the UK's rapidly changing constitutional landscape, in which many new opportunities for democratic participation are opening up. The impact of new information technologies will change our view of what resources we need to act as responsible citizens. And fundamentally, a far-reaching debate is beginning over *citizenship and welfare*, focusing on a new balance between rights and responsibilities. Citizenship has numerous dimensions:

- legal – the framework of enforceable rights;
- social and cultural – the rights and responsibilities that secure social cohesion, democratic participation, and balanced personal development;
- informational – the scope for access to the information and advice needed to make the most of rights and responsibilities;
- economic – concerning access to a level of income allowing for the exercise of rights and responsibilities and a decent standard of living, and concerning the contributions required to be eligible for forms of welfare support.

In the past fifteen years there has been more debate over people's rights and capacities as *consumers* than as citizens. The current wave of discussion and argument over the development of education for citizenship, and over the rediscovery of mutuality as a philosophy of reciprocal rights and civic responsibilities,[54] represents a reaction against the narrowing of the conception of the citizen during the 1980s and early 1990s. Gradually, the UK is developing a formal framework for citizens' rights and is beginning to overhaul the welfare system on the basis of a new idea of entitlements to benefit and reciprocal responsibilities to make self-provision against risk.

But there is a vast amount of debate and policy development still to take place. This opens up opportunities for disabled people and campaign bodies to make innovative interventions. In particular, we need a richer debate on what counts as a *social contribution* which can make a valid claim, in the spirit of mutuality, on welfare support. If this is defined solely in terms of mainstream paid work, then many people, not only disabled citizens, may face new forms of stigma and exclusion as well as new openings through government policy changes; but if it is defined more widely to embrace volunteering, caring and other contributions to social capital, then new routes to an inclusive future could open up.

The idea of mutuality, discussed in chapter 1, can be invoked in radical ways here. It would underline the argument promoted by government that rights imply responsibilities; and it would go beyond this statement by observing that *fulfilling responsibilities requires in many cases an extension of rights or tougher measures to make them a reality*. For disability policy this could mean an acceptance of the argument that all who can contribute to society through work should do so – but that for disabled people to do this demands that *they be enabled through comprehensive provision of equal access in workplaces and enforcement of disability equal rights*.

We consider some of the key elements of the emerging debates, risks and opportunities below.

Four key issues are highlighted in the following sections: first, the impact of the Disability Rights Commission (DRC); second, the impact of new interactive digital information systems and digital television; third, the growth in opportunities for democratic participation; and fourth, the benefits system.

2.2 Disability Rights Commission

The establishment of the DRC sends a powerful signal to employers and society as a whole that because disabled people's rights have not been sufficiently observed, legislation has been created which will be enforced. The DRC could mark out a distinctive position by promoting an inclusive and innovative approach to the social model of disability and to corporate social responsibility, as suggested above, alongside its role as a watchdog and enforcer. The scope for promoting and using greater levels of public understanding and empathy is potentially greater than in the case of women's equality – which seems a hard concept for some men to grasp even now – and racial equality, which is still a problematic concept for many in the white population. As noted in the introduction, disability is not a separate category which others cannot enter, it is a common experience in anyone's life, whether through personal impairment or that of a friend or relative or colleague. It also cuts across other fields of inequality and injustice – race, age and gender – and *intensifies* the disadvantage in these areas.

In establishing an agenda for its first decade, the DRC can build on the potential for empathy, identification and a sense of shared concerns, and will increasingly be able to point to role models in senior 'mainstream' positions who work effectively – all of which can boost the citizenship status of disabled people. However, role models have been available for many years, and there is also a need for senior figures in society to take a high-profile lead in calling for positive attitudes towards disability on the part of the non-disabled. MORI research for Scope in 1998 showed that 86 per cent of the public agreed that prominent figures in society 'should show a positive attitude to disabled people' to help break down discrimination and negative perceptions about disabled people.

The DRC will also be operating in the midst of rhetoric and developing practice in government which favours 'joined up thinking' and 'joined up solutions' in order to tackle deep-seated and complex social problems that cut across many public agencies and policy areas. 'Holistic government' is counterposed to fragmented and departmentalised solutions which often simply displace problems or make them worse. Fragmentation of communication, dumping of problem cases and inconsistent policy between employment, health and social services practitioners are common experiences of many disabled people and their carers, and overcoming this is a key element of the new strategy for carers announced in February 1999 by the government.[55] So far disability policy has not been joined up enough:[56] the Social Exclusion Unit, the flagship innovation to date in holistic policy-making, does not tackle disability, which is 'owned' in Whitehall mainly by the DfEE; and the complex assessment processes for disability benefits are a classic example of non-joined-up policy.

The DRC could take a lead in assessing policies on disability and social exclusion against the aims of 'joined up government' for more co-ordinated approaches by central government departments, public agencies at national, regional and local levels, and for more unified, one-stop approaches to delivering policies to people which are designed to make sense for the individual rather than for the service providers. It could also be a key partner with other disability organisations in building on Marilyn Howard's important recommendation of a National Disability Strategy, helping create a blueprint which fits into government's wider programme for social reform and modernising Britain.[57]

The DRC will be in a position to monitor and highlight success stories and shortcomings in the push for joined-up policies in public services, and solutions found in meeting the needs of disabled people and carers are likely to contain lessons which are widely applicable for other groups. This points to the great scope that exists for common action by the equal opportunities agencies in the UK.

The DRC will also inevitably become involved in the complexities of debate over the linkages and tensions between a rights-based approach to disability and the traditional benefits-based approach, which, as Helen Bolderson has noted, treats disability as an administrative category. Tensions between universal citizenship rights and increasingly targeted and conditional benefits are likely to be highlighted as the UK's debate on civil rights evolves and as welfare reform proceeds.

The DRC can also play a role in helping disability campaign bodies adapt to the changing environment of work, learning, citizenship and technology. As in other areas of equal rights campaigning, disability organisations have become very diverse in their approaches to lobbying and informing the public and decision-makers, and inevitably clashes occur between styles of argument and campaigning. Just as in women's movements and race equality movements, there is a gap between the radical direct action campaigners who celebrate their difference while calling for equality, and those who place most emphasis on winning equality in the 'mainstream' and downplay differences with the 'majority' population. The risk for the radical parts of the disability lobby is that, for all their achievements, passion and effectiveness, they could become alienated from its more conventional counterparts – a familiar development in other equal rights cultures – and will find it hard to make valuable alliances with other causes.

Does this mean that radical campaign groups are somehow 'outdated'? No: in every area of policy we need campaigners with 'maximal' demands and far-reaching arguments who push the boundaries of debate and help make a climate for change. And we also need campaigns that can weave a story about change that fits the prevailing vision of policy-makers in government. At the moment, and probably for a considerable time to come, that will be about modernisation, social inclusion through work, consensus-building, partnerships, and mutual rights and responsibilities. Campaigners need to exploit the opportunities that the government's long-term programme throws up, as well as highlight its failings.

Our argument has been that an inclusive future can be made if we recognise more the common cause between disabled people and the non-disabled who are at risk of exclusion. This implies more campaigning across the cultures of equal rights lobbying, and more partnerships between campaigners and employers, campaigners and public agencies, campaigners and policy-makers – as we have seen in recent years in many fields of NGO activity such as the environment. The DRC could act as a broker between the different 'equal rights cultures' and a catalyst for partnerships to promote social inclusion across boundaries. It could, for example, set up an *annual equal rights summit* between itself, the EOC and the CRE, and bring into this mutual learning event policy-makers, employers, campaigners against age discrimination and other forms of prejudice, for the development of new contacts and partnerships, and the sharing of ideas.

Finally, the DRC can play a key role in promoting and helping implement joined-up policy-making in support of social inclusion. This has four elements: stimulating culture changes in business, government, education and wider society to combat prejudice; focusing on tools to measure outcomes of policy so that we have meaningful measures of progress to an inclusive future; looking at the impact of policies across traditional departmental boundaries to ensure that unintended problems are reduced or eliminated; and taking a preventive and therefore anticipatory approach to discussing the challenges of the future which affect disabled people's life chances. This last role may be the most important, and the most controversial, when we consider the potential that exists not only for greater inclusion in future but also for further forms of *exclusion*.

A complex and profound example of the kind of issue which the DRC and its partners will need to explore in this anticipatory and preventive way of thinking is the rise of human genetics research and innovation in medical technology. There is, for example, growing debate on the ethics of new technologies for managing human fertility and the survival of the very ill – an intensely controversial issue highlighted in the BMA's 1999 guidelines on decisions to end treatment for patients in extreme cases of sickness and low quality of life. Who decides, and on what basis, how we should proceed with new techniques and the ethical dilemmas they give rise to? The issues are highly relevant to public perceptions of disability and inclusion/exclusion. They raise important questions about the impact of new technologies in medicine and fertility on our views of impairments and the extent to which they should be accepted or 'overcome' medically.

Consider the possibilities opened up by new knowledge of the human genetic code and by new medical technologies. Suppose we can eventually prevent some forms of impairment. Is there a danger that those who still have such impairments will face even more social exclusion and identification as 'disabled'? And what if we find ways of overcoming severe impairments such as paraplegic conditions? This might be termed the 'Christopher Reeve question': the paralysed actor's determination to walk again has aroused fierce debate among disability campaigners. If he does not accept his impairment, is he implicitly reinforcing society's view of it as something that makes him less than equal, even less than fully human? And what about disabled people who wish to accept their impairment as part of what they are, and to be treated as equal citizens? If they refuse to take advantage of some form of new treatment of their impairment, will they face incomprehension and intensified 'excluding attitudes' from the non-disabled? Will we, gradually, be influenced by the emergence of new genetic and medical techniques subconsciously to discriminate *even more* against 'the disabled' who can't or won't be 'treated'?

To many people outside the disability movement such questions and forebodings might sound histrionic or implausible. But the implications of the new genetics and medical ethics are such that these questions will need to be faced and debated openly. The DRC will need to help stimulate debate and learning in this emerging area of innovation, controversy and doubt.

2.3 Information and inclusion

Access to information and citizenship are closely related. With the rise of the Internet and personal computer, fears have grown of a new form of social exclusion – 'information exclusion'. Those on low incomes or in isolated conditions could be left marginalised by the information revolution as it enters a new phase of innovation and expansion:

- people in the lower income groups have less access to PCs and the Internet than do those in the ABC1 categories;
- the well-educated and higher-skilled workers are more likely to be owners of PCs and users of Internet links at home and at work than are those in lower level work or on low incomes;
- the cost of a basic PC kit (computer, printer, software) is unlikely to fall much below the £500-1000 level, and even if lower cost kits are produced the speed of software development may make many of them unsuitable for certain applications; moreover, the running costs of basic kits – especially of Internet use – can still be high;
- the elderly, those in rural areas and those in ethnic minorities are less likely to own or use new IT systems than the younger age groups, those in cities and in the white population;
- disabled people on low incomes and out of work are very unlikely to have regular access to new IT systems;
- innovations in IT-based marketing allow companies to 'red-line' low-income households deemed unlikely to be customers for products or services;

- much contact with IT is gained through work: those out of work are likely to miss out on opportunities to gain skills and confidence.

Against this picture, developments over the next decade offer huge scope for inclusion of currently excluded people, especially perhaps disabled people:

- the development of truly low-cost computers – cut-down PCs or terminals offering access to services such as word-processing over the Internet;
- the increased power of the Internet as a mechanism for information exchange, job advertisement and application, links to public services (social security, health, education in particular), shopping and social contact – some 138 million people worldwide are expected by BT to be linked to the Net by 2001;
- the drive within government to make more services and information accessible remotely via the Internet in the next few years;
- the development of digital TV, with built-in e-mail and other basic interactive services – potentially allowing many people to by-pass the PC entirely;
- the promotion of free access to e-mail by Internet service providers, which could lead to a massive expansion in households' access to e-mail in the next few years;
- the development of increasingly fast and reliable means of communicating by computer through devices other than keyboard and mouse – voice-recognition, voice-activation, joystick, eye-movement recognition, Braille keyboards, touch screens, headsets and the like;
- the development of products to help overcome visual or other sensory impairment in using IT systems such as the Internet: for example, the BETSIE text-to-speech converter launched by BBC Education to improve Internet access for blind and visually impaired users (see www.bbc.co.uk/education);
- the development of many new telecommunications systems adapted to the needs of disabled people, such as BT's TypeTalk service for those with hearing impairments;

- the development of a wide variety of private and public means to access the Internet – PC, TV, telephone, public IT-based information points, community centres, cafes, schools, colleges and the like;
- the immense scope in a high turnover industry for recycling of outdated computers for use by voluntary and community organisations and by schools and those with very basic word-processing and calculation needs.

Issues to be addressed in relation to 'information inclusion' for disabled people converge with those arising for lower income and isolated groups generally:

- the availability of subsidies for low-income households for take-up of digital TV incorporating e-mail by as much of the population as possible in advance of the switching off of the analogue broadcast spectrum around 2010;
- the access of those out of work to regular use of IT systems and to skill development in using the Internet and major software systems;
- the need for attention not only to how government services can be made 'electronic' but also to how the users of the services – often low-income households – will have the means to access them when this is the most appropriate means of doing so;
- the need to avoid the risk that improved 'virtual inclusion' via electronic systems could *reduce motivation and resources* for tackling the exclusion designed into the physical environment and ingrained in public attitudes; virtual inclusion might be gained at the price of entering an 'electronic ghetto' with no real gains in social mixing and physical access;
- the development of integrated learning centres in the community (see section 1.3) which, like cyber-cafes, could offer low-cost or free Internet access to users, and which would incorporate a full range of disability adaptations;
- the availability of affordable IT adaptations to allow disabled people to make best use of systems and to remain in work;
- the securing of appropriate social investments in IT from major IT suppliers which will have a major stake in the 'wiring' of government and education and other public services;

- the pre-emptive design and adaptation of new systems (such as smart card systems for electronic cash transactions, IT kiosks) not only in relation to private sector services but also in public services, especially benefits, health and education, to meet the needs of disabled people, rather than their costly re-engineering at a later date;[58]
- the improved availability of IT services and training from community organisations, including schools and colleges, the proposed employee mutuals, and disability organisations (as provided, for example, by the RNIB);
- use of the expansion of channels and media by disability campaign and advice bodies and the DRC to increase the representation of disabled people in television, films and the arts in general, as called for by Lord David Putnam, Chair of the National Endowment for Science, Technology and the Arts, in his 1999 Leonard Cheshire Lecture. There has been a substantial advance in the frequency and range of women's and ethnic minority people's participation in the media – there should be great scope, given the proliferation of new channels – for DRC and others (such as the EFD's Broadcasters' Disability Network) to lobby for a similar advance for disabled people. A higher and more positive profile for disabled people in the media was one of the measures favoured by the opinion formers surveyed by Leonard Cheshire as a way to promote greater social inclusion.[59]

2.4 Democratic participation

The next decade will see many new opportunities for citizens to participate in the democratic process. This is a development that potentially opens up new scope for awareness-raising about disability and for disabled people to take greater part in policy-making and debate. As in other areas, the arrival of new processes and institutions in principle makes it possible to 'design in' disability awareness and access from the outset. Innovations we have already seen, will have or are likely to see by 2010 include:

- establishment of new elected assemblies in Scotland and Wales;
- establishment of directly elected mayors in UK cities;

- a reformed second chamber of Parliament;
- Regional Development Agencies and Chambers, possibly evolving within the decade to form elected regional assemblies and executives;
- many efforts to modernise local authorities and find new ways to improve public participation, including perhaps new neighbourhood councils, electronic voting over the Internet, weekend elections, new community fora, and so on;
- the introduction of the Best Value system in local government to govern purchasing policy and assessment of service quality;
- more systematic promotion of civic and moral education in the school curriculum;
- new attempts to improve public confidence and participation in the land use planning system, including perhaps the development of neighbourhood plans devised by planners and local people;
- many uses for citizens' juries and similar consensus-building events in framing controversial questions and exploring attitudes and solutions to them.[60]

A feature of the debate on democratic modernisation has been the desire for innovations which can capture public imagination, increase trust and confidence in institutions, and break with the 'Westminster' and 'municipal' models. Parliament and local councils are associated by many with remoteness, stuffy ceremony and bizarre working arrangements wholly out of line with modern work practices and a sane family life. New institutions and processes could – with pressure from campaigners and the DRC – design in from the beginning arrangements which will maximise the opportunity for disabled people not only to vote or be consulted but also to stand for election or be nominated for consultative office. All such developments would highlight disability issues and make them visible and everyday for non-disabled people in new fora of every kind. Possible developments include:

- new assembly chambers and consultation fora with full disability access, and equipped as standard with disability support services within and without (such as plentiful parking for disabled people);

- free public transport services to such assembly centres – and new services well-equipped for disabled people's needs;
- introduction of quotas for representation of different social groups in a second chamber of Parliament, which would include a guaranteed representation of disabled people and non-disabled advocates;
- similar arrangements for any new chambers at regional level could be imagined;
- the introduction of a citizens' jury element in all chambers – with a portion of places reserved for non-voting consultative representatives, chosen by lot for 'democratic jury service'. This has been proposed by Barnett and Carty for House of Lords reform: a representative portion of new 'people's peers' would be selected by lot with quotas by gender, region, race, disability and so on, and would serve for say three to six months, with compensation to employers and payment for their time, with a guarantee of return to their previous job if they had one;[61]
- as proposed by campaigners for members of the new Scottish parliament, *job-sharing* could be introduced for elected members in order to boost representation of groups deterred by the time demands of service as representatives. This could be allowed for either as a joint slate for election or as a component of party lists in the proportional voting systems now gaining ground. Again, this innovation could benefit disabled people as well as other groups under-represented in current assemblies;
- many new forms of consultation, debate and direct lobbying at all levels of the new UK democratic system can be imagined via the Internet. This will be a key area for development by disability NGOs, and innovative means of funding initiatives by community organisations and other NGOs will need to be devised to tap the potential;
- involvement of disabled people as designers of policy – for example of disability equality training, new assessment processes and Best Value plans – and encourage staff swaps between public agencies and departments in Whitehall and disability bodies;[62]
- new forms of performance indicators, often developed by authorities in consultation with local communities, will proliferate as

policy-makers seek more 'joined up' measures of outcomes rather than simply inputs and outputs. There are many opportunities here for the DRC and disability campaigners to make a contribution which will build in disability access and satisfaction measures to new indicators of local and national development (see also section 1.3 on learning).

In the short term, as noted in research by Scope, there are serious access problems for disabled people when voting in elections.[63] It also found that 94 per cent of polling stations had access problems. This underlines the need for existing buildings used for democratic participation to be brought up to high standards of access for disabled people as a matter of urgency. Analyses by Scope of the 1997 General Election campaign showed that neither the parties, the candidates, election material nor the media paid significant attention to issues that may directly affect disabled people.[64] Innovations of the kind listed above could go some way, in tandem with other measures, to redressing this plainly inequitable and unacceptable situation.

2.5 Benefits and income

Given the employment disadvantages of many disabled people, and the care needs that many of them have, a fundamental component of citizenship is adequate income via benefits if not through paid work or a mixture of the two. Without this no one can gain the increase in *independence of living* which is a key aspiration and yardstick of inclusion for many disabled people.

The current policy environment is still taking shape. It contains several elements whose ultimate nature and effect are far from clear:

- changes in pensions policy, with the possibility of new forms of second pension for disabled people and for carers;
- severe pressure on local social services and health care budgets, with more charges being introduced for disability services;
- a continuing run-down in the value of the state pension;
- increased emphasis on the principle that *many benefits are dependent on willingness to prepare for and take paid work* – and uncertainty about

the degree to which state-backed work will be available in the absence of sufficient private sector job creation;

- a related risk of stigma and intensified marginalisation for people who face special problems in getting into officially recognised forms of work – a particular issue for people with learning disabilities;
- the need to ensure that a decent standard of living via the welfare system is available to those unable to enter work – especially for elderly people at rising risk of long-term illness and impairment;
- uncertainty about how to tackle benefits and poverty traps which provide disincentives to work or to gain pay rises – as shown by research by the Joseph Rowntree Foundation, accentuated in the case of many severely disabled people by the 'care trap' whereby disabled people in work face so many problems in making personal assistance arrangements that employment becomes an untenable option;[65]
- uncertainties about the balance between targeting and universalism in the reformed welfare state envisaged by the government;
- a lack of clarity about how government can achieve its aims to tackle poverty and end child poverty over a generation without higher benefit levels for those unable to work and a greater degree of redistribution, especially given the rejection of income tax increases to fund improved public services and benefits;[66]
- a search for new taxes (like the windfall tax) to pay for policy innovations.

Inadequate income and dependence on personal fund-raising among those in work or out of it clearly limit independence and result in less than inclusive citizenship. Other problems arise too. Research for Scope in 1998 found that 76 per cent of respondents had problems with their disability aids, one-third had to raise the money for better aids themselves or through charities – and 39 per cent could not manage without such equipment.[67]

A key question concerning benefits, inclusion and citizenship is whether forms of benefit can be devised which do not stigmatise the recipient or place them obviously in an 'excluded' ghetto category. This is of course not only a problem affecting disabled people. In the face of the uncertainties surrounding the reform of welfare, it is hard to forecast how benefits might change. The core principle now in place is that there should be work for those who can get jobs or enter self-employment, and that there should be security for those who cannot work. But many questions remain.

For many disabled people the move from welfare to work cannot be a quick one: carefully managed transitions may be needed in many cases from residential or hospital settings, and allowance must be made for flexible moves from work to benefits if a job opportunity goes wrong or is short term.[68] Is the welfare-to-work system truly geared to a world of flexible working and complex transitions to and from work? As Lunt and Thornton put it, *'Flexible working clearly requires flexible benefits'*.

It seems clear that we will have to see yet more radical reforms of the welfare state, and in particular of the relationship between work and benefits, if the principle of welfare-to-work is to be sustainable, not only for disabled people but for many other citizens as well. The changes in the labour market outlined earlier make a more flexible and creative approach to welfare-to-work essential over the long run, and this is a *universal* issue, not one specific to disabled people. We suggest that the following developments could be seen towards 2010 as policy-makers attempt to rethink welfare and its links to work and citizenship:

- a redefinition of what counts as 'work' and 'contribution to society' in relation to income support and welfare-to-work strategies, underpinned by an ethos of mutuality and reciprocal rights and responsibilities – including full recognition of caring as a service which saves the state immense sums and is massively under-invested at present;
- further moves to recognise volunteering as a form of 'actively seeking work', and a search for more creative means of mixing income from work (mainstream and casual) and benefits, with changes to taper mechanisms (for example, tapering over time rather than by earnings disregards) to build in 'buffer' periods to counter benefit and poverty trap effects;[69]
- in relation to this, more means of combining voluntary work with benefits of varying kinds and with paid work and learning in 'portfolios' of activity, possibly with benefit credits built up in the form of 'Active Citizen's Credits';[70]

- localised experiments in new forms of benefit and work portfolios, perhaps with intermediate organisations such as the employee mutual acting as benefit administrators;
- a unified approach to assessment of benefit eligibility, focusing on employability and real partnership with the disabled claimant in designing a package of benefits and plans for work and learning;[71]
- much more effective 'joining up' of money, advice, information and access services affecting disabled people, integrating employment advisors, benefits assistance, learning advice and housing assistance, and better integration between public and voluntary services to assist disabled people;
- more examination of ways to guarantee a decent income to people unable to achieve it through work or personal savings as a result of disability: Helen Bolderson has suggested that there is a need to explore a 'compensation' or 'reparation' model for benefits that takes into account 'socially imposed' loss of amenity experienced by disabled people; she also notes the scope for *increasing individual customisation* of welfare services around needs and capabilities, potentially facilitated by new IT systems, and potentially also reducing stigma and pigeon-holing of disabled people as a group defined by negative attributes (that is, by what they can't do rather than what needs and capacities they have);[72]
- appropriate payment – which would be disregarded for benefit purposes – for time and commitment from disabled people participating in consultative exercises, such as representing views of service users; this could take the form of cash payments or credits;
- more delivery of benefits via electronic links (promoted also by the advent over the next ten to fifteen years of 'digital money' or 'e-cash' systems), whether to the home or an intermediate place (such as an employee mutual) could help to reduce the perceived stigma of benefit receipt, as could more opportunities for mixing benefits with work, learning, volunteering and so on;
- the idea of intermediate bodies as payers of flexible benefits packages to people who are unemployed and seeking ways of working or training while meeting other needs and responsibilities could be a way of overcoming stigma, as could the very existence of such routine means of combining benefit with other forms of income;[73]

- new developments in outcome indicators, social impact assessment in business and 'holistic auditing' in government could help in the gradual process of re-evaluating the value to the taxpayer and community of particular activities (such as caring and childcare) and making provision of benefits-for-activity more publicly a matter of social *investment* rather than social 'handouts';[74]
- finally, we need much more involvement of disabled people and disability organisations in designing research on work and benefits experience, in designing and appraising assessment procedures, and in seeking a unified approach to assessments as part of the single gateway for claimants.[75]

2.6 Conclusions: action for inclusion

The establishment of the DRC, the rise of new information technologies, the modernisation of democratic institutions and the reform of welfare all open up big opportunities for promoting the social inclusion of disabled people. But inclusion will not happen automatically as a result of these developments. The DRC will have a pivotal role in pushing for equal citizenship rights for disabled people and also in promoting solutions which recognise common cause between disabled and non-disabled people and the benefits to all that can come from redesigning services and environments for disability equality. It should hold an annual summit of all the equality agencies and their partners which will develop common policy goals to be promoted to government, business and other sectors.

Key issues concerning citizenship include the success of attempts to 'join up' policy-making at all levels and the reform of welfare services. The DRC and partners across the disability world and beyond need to hold government to account in achieving co-ordinated policies on exclusion in general and on disability in particular. They should build on Howard's recommendations for a National Disability Strategy incorporating new cross-cutting policy bodies in government.[76] The DRC and its partners should also campaign to ensure that all the new bodies in UK governance and all the new initiatives for service improvement and public consultation take full account of disability rights and inclusion. For example, pressure needs to be brought to bear on the Regional Development Agencies and the design of the Best Value system in local government to ensure that disability issues are firmly established in mainstream policy-making and planning.

Above all, we need a far-reaching debate, facilitated by disability bodies and other campaigners on exclusion and inclusion, on the limits of current welfare reform approaches. This would highlight the need for much more radical and flexible approaches to defining 'work' and 'contributions' and to designing new packages of work *and* benefits appropriate to the conditions of the labour market and people's capacities to contribute to society. Disability bodies should form partnerships with others in the social justice field and with the DRC to develop a blueprint for welfare reform which will build on the current modernisation policies and improve them, and promote these strongly to government.

3. Design for life
The built environment and new technology

3.1 Introduction
The modernisation of the UK is not simply about the introduction of new constitutional arrangements, policies and rights and responsibilities. The prospects for greater inclusion of disabled people will be significantly affected by the modernisation of the environment. Renewal of the fabric of towns and cities and the introduction of new infrastructures – physical and virtual – for communication will not come quickly in many areas. However, there is a fair chance that by 2020 the UK will have rewired its telecommunications and television systems, built millions of new homes, renovated many rundown communities and gone a long way to dealing with the immense investment backlog in public transport.

The modernisation programmes that lie ahead offer great opportunities to build in disability access and rights for disabled people that were ignored in previous phases of designing for life in the UK. They also open up a wider opportunity for 'universal' or 'inclusive' design – approaches to design of everyday products and infrastructures that benefit not only disabled people but also many who are not disabled. Once again, a 'mutualist' agenda could be opened up.

This chapter picks up themes from the previous discussions in considering the potential of new technologies in information systems, disability aids and home design. It also looks at the scope for overcoming the extreme exclusion for disabled people generated by the shortcomings of design in the built environment, including the public transport system.

The design of everyday infrastructures systematically undermines independence and inclusion for disabled people. Most seriously, there are many disabled people on low incomes living in poor-quality housing with bad facilities for access. Full enforcement of access standards only applies to new-build housing and buildings undergoing 'substantial' retrofitting. Gerry Zarb notes that, 'Consequently, people who do not have the resources to purchase new homes will be faced with only two choices: either stay put in inaccessible housing or, if they are able, to move to new-build social housing. Neither of these options are of course inclusive solutions: even if some people are able to gain access to suitable social housing they will still be excluded from the majority of other buildings'.[77]

The infrastructure of public and private transport is profoundly 'user-hostile' for disabled people. Although Railtrack reports that there has been a steady increase in the number of disabled passengers requesting assistance in using rail transport over the past five years, and a rise in the number of disabled persons' railcards issued,[78] this is unlikely to be a sign of satisfaction with the rail service on the part of disabled users. Much of UK public transport is in a shambolic state, unattractive, expensive, obstructive and inaccessible for disabled people: Audit Commission research on public transport indicates that planning of services for disabled people has yet to take full account of the DDA or of the government's push for a more integrated and sustainable transport policy; and there is little evidence yet of 'joined-up' work between public transport authorities and social services providing accessible transport services.[79]

Given the recognition by government that the transport systems are in bad repair, that the railways in particular are 'a national disgrace' (as stated by John Prescott), and that a sustainable transport strategy must aim for a much larger role for public transport modes, there is long-term hope for improvement. Railtrack and many other public transport providers are taking steps to improve disability access in particular and service quality in general.[80]

But the timetable stretches beyond 2010 for radically improved public transport access. Even DDA-inspired changes will take many years to come into effect: the Audit Commission states that it will be fifteen to twenty years before the bus fleet is fully compliant with the access requirements of the DDA. This has significant implications for disabled people's choices about transport access.

Access to the labour market for disabled people is closely linked to transport issues. Access is heavily dependent on the ease with which an individual can negotiate their built environment, and also on the affordability of support they might need. Scope found in 1994 that 58 per cent of its respondents overall, and over 70 per cent of wheelchair users, could not use buses easily, although 40 per cent of respondents had access to a car.[81] A further consideration is the ease with which people can live in their own homes. Lamb and Layzell found that, as well as experiencing financial constraints on buying essential aids, 40 per cent of respondents felt that their housing was insufficiently adapted to meet their needs.

The design of retail services is also problematic. The recent Grass Roots survey of some of the largest retail, food and financial services in the UK found that four out of five companies surveyed could not provide alternative formats for information that may have been more accessible to a disabled person.[82] The survey found that two in five wheelchair users had problems entering premises, and 70 per cent of profoundly deaf people in the survey reported that service staff could not meet their needs. Only one in three banks and building societies surveyed had made provision for hearing-impaired customers (such as induction loops) and the survey found that only half of the loop systems available were functioning. The study also uncovered organisational problems – for example, that in general retail service staff were insufficiently trained to deal with the needs of many disabled people, regardless of good intent.

This study covered many of the organisations with a good record of recognition at strategic level of the needs of disabled people, and it underlines the degree to which even relatively enlightened employers and service providers fall short of putting awareness into practice in the design of goods, services and access. There is a major need for more research and information about the real costs of adaptation of facilities, especially in the light of survey findings noted earlier that most disabled workers feel they do *not* need extensive adaptations to their workplace to do their job well, and that few firms in the scope of the DDA Part III mentioned cost as an obstacle to investing in adaptations or planning to do so.

Given the obvious backlog of investments in adaptations that will make buildings and transport systems more accessible, there is a temptation to place most hope for a more inclusive environment for disabled people in developments in the home. For example, many disabled people can gain great benefits from using new 'smart' computer-based household equipment and from new interactive digital information links, allowing tele-working, virtual travel, communication, shopping and so on.

While there is huge potential in the development of domestic IT and other aids, any temptation to see them as a panacea must be resisted: the digital revolution on its own will not deliver all the benefits of inclusion that we should hope for. For there is a risk, in effect, of confining many disabled people to the home even more than they presently are; and there is also the risk that emphasis on technological aids and adaptations in the home will distract attention from continuing inequalities in work and the wider environment affecting disabled people.

Moreover, disabled interviewees stress that many technological innovations are 'user-frivolous' rather than user-friendly. They do not get to the point of the frustrations experienced by many disabled people, and while they might offer more convenience or an alleviation of a problem, they do not *solve* the wider problem. A superbly adapted IT system might tell you all you need to know about a play you wish to see or a football match you wish to attend, but does little to compensate for the dismal level of disability access offered by the local theatre or football club.

A unifying theme in relation to 'design for life' trends and issues is that the key innovation over the next ten to fifteen years is not likely to be any particular change in technology or physical infrastructure, but rather *the increased capacity for disabled people in particular, and consumers in general, to become actively consulted as designers*, engaged in dialogues of various kinds before the event about what their needs, concerns and priorities are.

Is this likely? As before, we can identify a hopeful sign in the twin overall trends of modernisation of infrastructures and the search for public trust by institutions and businesses. Both are promoting moves for extensive public consultations and innovations in participative design (for example, focus group testing by business in product and service design, and exercises in democratising the planning system through innovations such as 'Planning for Real' consultations with local communities about their wishes for the design of their areas).

The scale of the modernisation and new development likely over the next fifteen years will combine with the need for trust-building to generate many opportunities for disability advocates to build in the disability access agenda from the start. It will also open up huge scope for development of the 'mutualist' agenda discussed in chapter 1 – arguments showing that taking disability access seriously does not benefit only disabled people but also the non-disabled.

This takes us away from seeing design for access as a 'minority issue' and towards a view that highlights *the wide range of people who can benefit from, and provide a market for, design features that help them use products and services more easily.* 'Universal access' as an ideal emphasises that many adaptations of consumer goods, for example, can find a *mass market* rather than be viewed as a costly concession to 'minority needs': an ageing society creates large markets for design options that will benefit people with impairments, whether they see themselves as 'disabled' or not.[83] An illustration of this way of thinking is given by Railtrack in its Disability Strategy consultation paper:

'The provision of an accessible rail network will benefit a much wider sector of the community than just disabled people. The three types of passengers that experience particular difficulties when using the rail network are:

1. disabled people;
2. elderly people, some of whom are disabled;
3. people who are 'temporarily encumbered', such as parents with pushchairs, people carrying heavy bags, people with broken limbs.'[84]

This is not to say that an approach based on more 'universal' thinking about access and design is a panacea. Conflicts over priorities will always arise, and 'universal access' design will always leave out the needs of some people with particular impairments, which will require specific attention. But recognising this does not detract from the key point that there is scope for regarding design for access as an issue which opens up a large common ground and common market linking the needs of disabled people and non-disabled consumers alike, especially against a backdrop of demographic change in a 'greying' society.

In relation to modernisation of infrastructures, opportunities will open up for *thorough redesign* in the period to 2010 in a number of ways, as outlined below.

3.2 Transport

There is a universally acknowledged need for massive investment in the public transport system, with billions of pounds to be invested in railway infrastructures and the London Tube system. Many access points are currently unusable by disabled people and designing in access from the start will be much more cost-effective than getting it wrong and then re-equipping stations. Given the problems of funding investment, change will be very slow unless access for disabled people is pre-emptively built into design of refurbished stations and trains and ticketing facilities.

The push from government on grounds of environmental sustainability, quality of life and economic efficiency for an 'integrated transport strategy' in principle opens up the possibility over the long term of many innovations to make life easier for disabled and non-disabled passengers alike on public transport. For example, we could see the introduction of booking door-to-door services through public transport providers (like taxi-rail-taxi, as available in the Netherlands) over the Internet or phone.

The government's long-term aim to implement an integrated and sustainable transport strategy also makes certain new policies to discourage car use and shift people on to public transport or virtual communications. Care will be needed to ensure that measures do not penalise disabled people whose main transport tool has to be an adapted car.

A key element in future sustainable and integrated transport policy will be the modernisation of bus systems, involving new fleets, new lanes and guided bus systems, and improved access and information services. This is because it is increasingly recognised that there are significant limitations on the rail system for absorbing new demand for travel and substituting for existing road use, and very large costs for infrastructure upgrades. Buses, by contrast, need few if any 'track upgrades', can be more flexible in routing and are more swiftly brought into service. Thus we can expect bus fleet redesigns on a large scale, and again it will be vital to ensure equal access for disabled people is designed in *at the beginning*, not just to buses but to stations, stops and information services.

3.3 Housing

In housing, there will be considerable investment in new homes and estates and possibly also in new towns, 'urban villages' and redevelopment of town centres and suburbs. The driver behind this is rising demand for new homes and for improvement of existing substandard stock: DETR estimates suggest that approximately 4 million new households will be created in the next fifteen to twenty years, and some estimates put the demand higher. Many of these households are likely to be for single people (young, divorced, widowed) and many of them, given the demographic shift towards a greyer population profile and smaller average household sizes in the next century, will be elderly. Many households will in addition be formed by disabled people with or without carers.[85]

Walker notes that the demographic projections and the household forecasts imply 'greater attention to care strategies for providers of social housing: the development perhaps of lifetime homes, more inter-agency working, more movement across the boundary between "general needs" and "supported housing".'[86] Leach argues that for many home-owning households the costs of paying for residential care for elderly relatives could be prohibitive.[87] As a result, more households might become multi-generational, implying a similar blurring of boundaries between 'general needs' design and 'special needs' adaptability.

An implication of such projections is an increase in demand for highly adaptable 'lifetime home' designs in new build and in house adaptations, making what seems at first a specialised model for disabled people into a potential *mainstream design choice* in future housing development and redevelopment.[88] Lifetime homes are designed for easy adaptation to a household's changing physical access needs, reducing the extent to which older people, for example, might be forced to move or to make expensive adaptations in the wake of disability or long-term illness. Again, this possible implication of wider social change over the next ten to fifteen years could become a focus for campaigning and public education by the DRC and disability organisations, with the effect of making common ground between disabled people's needs and those of the (as yet) non-disabled population, as suggested in the introduction.

The opportunity exists to influence the controversial national debate on meeting new housing demand and location, a debate which will run throughout the next decade at national, regional and local levels. The debate rages as to what proportion of new housing should be on greenfield sites in suburbs and the country as opposed to brownfield sites and redeveloped buildings in urban areas, and what densities, mixes of tenure and housing types should be aimed for. It seems likely that at least 40 per cent of new building will have to be on greenfield suburban and rural sites, raising the possibility – as promoted for example by the Town and Country Planning Association – of a need for *new settlements*.

This could mean the revival in a new form of garden cities or new towns, designed for the new century for sustainable urban living with a bias to mixed tenure and mixed-use developments, plentiful social housing with flexible rental packages and care service linkages, plentiful public transport, minimised need for car travel, mixed use developments and built-in excellence in access for disabled people. Lifetime home design *as a norm* could be a strong feature of any such developments, as could many innovations in urban layout. Such 'new new towns' would be a major demonstration of good practice in integrated design and promotion of flexible independent living for disabled people and non-disabled alike for established towns and cities to learn from.

But government targets for home building also aim at putting 60 per cent of new dwellings into 'brownfield' sites in towns and cities. This also opens up big opportunities for disability equality in 'design for life', as discussed next.

3.4 Urban design and planning

Three forces are driving a rethink of urban policy. First, the concentration of many of the worst social exclusion problems in the cities. Second, the related issue of flight to the suburbs and countryside by the affluent, a long-standing trend which generates huge pressures on rural land, adds to sprawl developments and traffic use and is associated with environmentally unsustainable trends. Third, the need to revive cities as a desirable place to live in order to avoid unsustainable land-take outside urban areas to meet projected demand for new homes.

These forces are behind John Prescott's stated intention to preside over a long-term 'urban renaissance' in the UK – a vision for which is set out in the report of Urban Task Force chaired by Lord Richard Rogers.[89] They are also behind the drive in many areas to check the development of edge-of-town retail developments – often accessible only by car – and revive urban centres where lower-income residents have often seen a decline in retail provision and quality of amenities. This major confluence of social trends and political pressures offers many potential benefits for disabled people.

The possible revival of new town building, and the push for improved public transport and redevelopment in town and city centres, and for 'urban villages' within conurbations, all point to large-scale opportunities for new design. There is a parallel trend within planning policy – itself now under systematic review by government and planning associations – to find new means of consulting the community about proposed and possible changes before they are decided upon. The aim is to boost public trust in and 'ownership' of new developments – for example, via 'Planning for Real' community participation exercises.

These trends open up scope for far more input from disabled people and disability organisations, especially in partnership with other agencies, which would promote safe, lively and diverse public spaces in which pedestrian and disability access would be paramount (see Figure 3 over).

Such changes chime with the ideas already noted about multiple uses for schools and colleges in chapter 1. They include: the promotion of multiple uses for buildings, bringing learning and communication centres into buildings with large 'waiting spaces' (termini, hospitals, GP centres, daycare centres, government offices); making streets places to linger, rest in, communicate from and learn in (for example, through more provision of group seating around kiosks and 'mini-stations' such as bus-stops, public IT service points, arcaded streets, and repopulation of public spaces with guards, attendants, concierges and wardens who

- virtual conferencing via video, audio or data (in Braille form, for instance), allowing 'virtual presence' in meetings which one cannot attend in person;
- improved prostheses and artificial limbs, more sophisticated disability aids of all kinds, and improved digital enhancement of impaired hearing, vision and speech – even, potentially in the long term, the restoration of sight or hearing through new implanted processors;
- improved and 'smarter' adapted vehicles.

Questions begged by such lists are many. How affordable will such devices be for disabled people? What subsidies will be available for their purchase? Is there a risk that such advances will be seen as 'solving the problem' of independence and access for people with disabilities? How closely involved will disabled people be in the design and development of such products and services? And in relation to the crucial issue of designing disability access into the standards for software systems and new digital communications services, how can we ensure that consumers' perspectives are understood and taken into account *before* new products and services are finalised and launched?[92] Kevin Carey notes that 'design for all' approaches which optimise product designs inclusively for a wide market of disabled and non-disabled people alike depend on much greater openness of processes for setting technical standards for new technology-based products and services. He argues that without prior consultations involving a recognition of the needs of the large marketplace of people experiencing disability, many major investments in infrastructure, such as the National Grid for Learning, will require expensive and complex 'retro-engineering' to adjust them for use by the growing population with impairments of various kinds and degrees of severity.

The development of such innovative goods and services as those listed above is either inevitable or at least highly likely in the next ten to fifteen years. They could promote big gains in well-being for many disabled people. However, if their benefits are to be harnessed to boost *social inclusion* as opposed to a narrow form of greater *domestic independence and convenience*, then a key development for the next decade will need to be closer involvement of disabled people in designing devices and services, and in linking such innovations to broader policy changes for the promotion of their inclusion as citizens in a modernised Britain. As Patricia Moore notes, design is crucial to creating an inclusive society, or in her words 'a healing environment' for the growing numbers of elderly people and those with impairments and who routinely experience disability reinforced through poor design.[93] But 'too many designers do what they think is the answer instead of finding out what people want'. Systematic processes for the inclusion of potential users of all ages and with special needs in product and service design are essential – and, as Carey notes, can open up large new markets which are being shaped by demographic changes but are currently disregarded and misunderstood by designers and marketeers.[94]

3.6 Conclusions: action for inclusion

The physical modernisation of the UK – in terms of transport, housing, estates, communications and domestic technologies – offers immense scope for taking disability access seriously and achieving a far more inclusive built environment. The key task is to ensure – via pressure from government, the DRC and disability bodies – that disability access is not a minority 'add-on' issue but an aspect of *universal design for mass markets*. Policies that should be pursued are:

- involving disabled people in design of new transport systems, environments, technologies and services from the very outset;
- building in 'universal design' or 'design for all' requirements to public purchasing and Best Value initiatives, and specifying user involvement in product and service design and assessment;
- establishing 'lifetime homes' design as a standard in new settlements to meet the home building projections over the next twenty years;
- exploring the scope for a mass retrofitting programme for low-income housing which would combine disability access with new insulation standards;
- new partnerships between disability organisations and campaigners and providers in other fields, such as planning, environment, IT, transport and housebuilding.

4. Conclusion

The process of 'modernisation' in many walks of life, driven variously by new policy directions (in welfare, devolution and public consultation, electronic government services, lifetime learning, educational standards, planning and outcome measurement), by globalisation, by business innovation in IT and by large-scale pressures of demographic and environmental change, opens up major opportunities for disabled people and their advocacy organisations.

The scale of *restructuring and new design* in society – organisational, technological and environmental – over the next ten years and more brings opportunities for positive change for disabled people in all circumstances. The establishment of new processes and institutions in principle makes it possible to 'design in' disability awareness and access from the outset and to dismantle 'disabling barriers' on a large scale. We suggest that this makes it possible to imagine a *new mutual interest* in access to services between disabled and non-disabled people. This recognition could be the starting point for creative policy-making, for innovative campaigning by disability organisations and their stakeholders, and for new thinking about 'universal' or 'inclusive' design of products and services by business. The key question for the next decade is how the potential – which is *unprecedented* – can be harnessed.

For nothing will happen automatically. The 'project of modernisation' needs constant vigilance and continuous improvement, and government needs the criticisms and recommendations of many bodies to advance the goals of social inclusion, democratic modernisation and infrastructural renewal. The DRC and disability campaigners have a huge range of opportunities ahead of them: they need to form powerful alliances across the field of social justice campaigning to make the most of them. The toolkit of modernisation – joined up policy on social exclusion, welfare to work, benefits reform, integrated transport, Best Value, devolution and so on – is flawed and incomplete, but it also offers much hope for progress and it is there to be improved and used vigorously. This report has highlighted many ways in which it could be done. If it is, then by 2010 we could be much nearer than we have ever been to an inclusive society with equal rights and fair opportunities for disabled people.

Appendix 1.

Notes on recent research on disability and employment

This appendix reviews some of the recent research material on disability and employment issues. The review makes no claims to completeness, and seeks to offer an overview of key issues and areas for further work.

As noted in the introduction, there are difficulties in measuring the extent of disability because of the wide span of impairments relevant to employment and the risk of social exclusion. There are also problems in gaining a picture of change over recent years in employment experience for disabled people. One of the problems in measuring the trends in employment patterns over time is that often the data are not comparable. This is because definitions of disability vary, there are different population bases used in research employing different reporting methods and a different understanding of what constitutes 'economic activity'. Finally, there are significant gaps or shortfalls in knowledge, and we provide a checklist of questions on which it is suggested that further research may be needed.

Despite the problems, some important and clear patterns emerge. The following data are drawn from the autumn 1998 findings of the Labour Force Survey (LFS), the UK's premier dataset on employment:[95]

- disabled people account for nearly 20 per cent of the working age population but for only about 11 per cent of all in employment, and employment rates vary greatly by type of disability;
- there are 2.8 million disabled people in employment: they are more likely than are non-disabled workers to be in part-time jobs or self-employment; it is unclear how far this reflects choice or limited options for gaining full-time employment with an employer;

- disability levels rise with age, with just under one-third of those in the 50 to 59 age group reporting a current long-term disability or health problem compared to just 10 per cent of those in the 20 to 29 age band;
- disabled people are seven times as likely as non-disabled people to be out of work and claiming benefits;
- disabled people in employment are three times as likely as others to receive state benefits (12 per cent compared with 4 per cent);
- over 1 million people with disabilities who are out of work would like to be in work – although the majority would not be able to start work immediately if it were available;
- disabled people are more likely to be long-term unemployed than are non-disabled people (39 per cent compared with 25 per cent);
- nearly 2 million long-term disabled people are economically inactive and *not* wanting employment;
- disabled people are more than twice as likely on average than non-disabled people to have no formal qualifications;
- unemployment rates (on the ILO definition – jobless, ready to start work in a fortnight and having looked for work in the last four weeks) are nearly twice as high for long-term disabled people (10.7 per cent) compared to non-disabled people (5.7 per cent).

Research data underline the differences between categories of disability as well as between disabled people and the non-disabled as a whole. Only 15 per cent of those with mental health problems, and 28 per cent of those with severe or specific learning difficulties, are economically active compared to 57 per cent of those who were visually impaired and 64 per cent of those with hearing difficulties.[96] This marked difference for those with hearing difficulties is shown in related data which suggest that the public views deafness as slightly different from other disabilities.

Unemployment rates for disabled people overall are greater than for the non-disabled, but those with learning difficulties have a rate of 25.8 per cent, those with mental health problems have an unemployment rate (using the ILO definition) of 22.1 per cent, and those with hearing difficulties have a rate of 12.3 per cent.[97] The gaps widen in relation to gender and age variables. Younger disabled people aged 25 to 34 are three times more likely to be unemployed than the non-disabled.[98] This survey also showed that whereas 11 per cent of the sample (aged over fifteen) were disabled, for those 'out of work' the figure rose to 18 per cent. But there are problems with extracting too much from these data: the data set covers those aged fifteen or older whereas other sources use different age categories. The term 'out of work' is insufficiently clear. Still, the case that disabled people are disadvantaged on a large scale in relation to employment is convincing.

The likelihood of unemployment is dependent on the severity and number of impairments an individual has. ONS data covering early 1996 are based on surveys covering those who have had a disability in the past and which ask whether this disability affects their ability to work. Research indicates that two-thirds of those with only one functional problem are in work, compared to 40 per cent of the working age disabled population with more than one such problem.

There is a distinction – not always evident in the research literature – between the disadvantages that may be faced by those who have been disabled from birth or a very young age, who perhaps have a congenital disability and those whose disability is acquired later in life. The majority (70 per cent) of economically active disabled people became disabled *while in work*, a significant fact which does not always seem to be made clear to the general public. For them, retaining their jobs once they have become disabled is a priority. Barnes et al cite a 1993 study in Devon by Hyde and Howes, which found that 61 per cent of those who became disabled while in work subsequently left for health reasons while over half claimed to have been dismissed or pressured into resigning.[99] Other data suggest that 55 per cent of disabled people feel in danger of losing their job because of their impairment.[100]

Being in work is more than just about financial security, but also about quality of life. A consultation by BMRB International for Scope in 1994 found that 82 per cent of disabled people in work described themselves as happy as compared to 57 per cent of those seeking work.[101] It also found, unsurprisingly, that those who were working had higher incomes and that they were less likely to say that they did not have as fulfilling a social life as they would like.

It is unsurprising therefore that many disabled people surveyed by Knight and Brent appear to approach employers with apprehension (note that this sample tends to over-represent those with severe disabilities). Eighty-six per cent of respondents who were seeking work feared they would be unsuccessful.[102]

How much does disadvantage reflect discrimination against disabled people? Lamb and Layzell report that, in their sample, 85 per cent of disabled people seeking work believed that employers were reluctant to offer them work because of their disability, and 51 per cent felt they had been refused an interview or job for work they were qualified for.[103] Thirty-one per cent of those in work felt they were over-qualified, and 44 per cent felt they did not have the same opportunities for promotion as the non-disabled. Seventy-eight per cent of disabled people say that they find it more difficult to change jobs than others.

A somewhat more positive picture emerges from some of the findings of the large survey by Meager et al for the DfEE.[104] This survey of 2,000 disabled people of working age found that unemployed people with disabilities generally had a positive outlook on finding work, agreeing strongly that a job was important to them and that they planned to continue their job search. The survey also found that just one in six of those who are or had been economically active said that they had been given unfair treatment or had suffered discrimination from an employer or potential employer in an employment-related context. Modifying this relatively encouraging picture is the finding that more than one quarter of disabled people who left their job because of their impairment said that suitable adaptations would have let them stay in work, but fewer than one in five said that they had been offered such modifications by the employer.

How can these divergent results on perceived discrimination be reconciled? Meager, commenting on IES research on DDA-based recruitment discrimination cases, argues that many disabled people are conditioned to have low expectations of their labour market experience and so are less likely than might be expected to identify discrimination.[105] Another explanation for the discrepancy is the gap between self-reported experience of discrimination and actual prejudice which is hidden to the individual job applicant because it is 'institutional'. Not every rejection will be experienced as an act of discrimination, but many might be nonetheless. The other side of the coin, complicating the issue further, is that some perceptions of discrimination might not correspond to an actual instance of discrimination.

Discrimination, like 'disability' itself, is bound to be a research subject which generates a wide range of estimates of its prevalence. Consider some of the forms it can take:

- based on a medical definition of disability;
- self-reported perception of being discriminated against;
- legally proven discrimination;
- perceived discrimination which is the subject of legal action;
- discrimination based on physical design (of a building, for instance);
- instituitionalised (that is, conscious and unconscious discrimination embedded in practices of an organisation);
- non-reported discrimination which is nonetheless felt by a disabled person.

Measurement in this context is very hard, and reliance on self-reported experience of discrimination needs to be complemented by attempts to construct objective indicators of discrimination and progress towards overcoming it.[106] A recent unpublished DfEE review of the varying research findings on discrimination suggests the following conclusion:

'there are clear and consistent differences in the labour market position of disabled people and others: disabled people are clearly disadvantaged across a range of outcomes. However, evidence of discrimination is rather less tangible: there appears to be little discrimination in recruitment and employment ... Perceived discrimination is likewise comparatively rare.'[107]

Even though discrimination is not necessarily perceived to be widespread on the basis of large-scale surveys, this does not diminish the reality of the disadvantage experienced in the labour market and in the workplace by many disabled people. Whether based on conscious discrimination or not, the evident reality of disadvantage raises the issue of employers' attitudes and practices. The 1996 Multi-purpose Survey of Employers found that 45 per cent of those covered by the DDA had a formal policy on the employment of disabled people. However, this may be covered in an overall equal opportunities policy, which may place more emphasis on ethnicity and gender: a further survey in 1996 for the DfEE found that only 17 per cent of employers had specific policies on disability.[108]

These results suggest a very divergent and often incomplete appreciation of the DDA, of the needs of disabled people and of the scope for access by them to the workplace on the part of many employers. This is backed up by the results of the baseline survey of organisations in the scope of the DDA Part III provisions, carried out in 1997 for the NDC by IES.[109] This found that just under half the 1,500 establishments surveyed had not made any changes at all to improve access for disabled people, with most believing that none were necessary and that they had a high level of awareness of the requirements of the DDA. Yet few had carried out any audit of provision, most were not planning to do so; over half had not consulted disabled customers about access issues and did not intend to. Few displayed detailed awareness of particular provisions of the Act, and over 60 per cent had not sought information, or did not intend to seek it, on the DDA. Large establishments and public sector bodies seemed to have a better record than others.

Research by Barnes et al found that the two obstacles to progress in the labour market which were of special concern in consultations with people with disabilities were inadequacies in education and problems generated by the benefits system.[110] Those who attended special schools may have experienced emotional, physical and educational segregation that impairs communication skills and workplace relations. Also it is possible that standards at particular special schools may not match those in mainstream education. Those who have spent long periods in hospital away from educational settings may have poor literacy and numeracy standards. There may also be inadequate access to resources in higher education. The benefits system presents the familiar barriers of the poverty and unemployment traps. Additional obstacles might include a demotivating attitude on the part of social security advisors, and a risk for some disabled people of being rejected for disability benefits and yet also rejected by employers on grounds of specific impairments and illnesses.

These discouraging findings also relate to those who care for and live with disabled people. Research carried out for Scope in 1994 found that only 31 per cent of carers who responded were in paid employment: disaggregating the sample showed that 13 per cent were full-time workers whereas 18 per cent were part time. 30 per cent of men combined full-time work with caring as opposed to 9 per cent of women, while 21 per cent of women were part-time workers compared to 7 per cent of men. Fifty per cent of carers who are not working left work because of their responsibilities.[111] Fifty-seven per cent of respondents in this study suggested they had been in financial difficulties as a result of their caring responsibilities, while 45 per cent had stopped saving, 25 per cent had delayed paying bills, 24 per cent had borrowed money and 22 per cent had bought more on credit.

Gaps in knowledge and limitations of available research

Finally, we list some of the limitations of existing research and gaps in knowledge apparent from the review of literature to date. A great deal of rigorous, substantial and informative research is carried out, notably on behalf of the DfEE, and important research is carried out by bodies such as the NDC, Leonard Cheshire Foundation, Scope, RNIB, RNID, Joseph Rowntree Foundation, the City University Rehabilitation Resource Centre and others. However, numerous limitations and gaps are apparent from a reading of recent material and we outline these below.

- A key problem, frequently mentioned by disability campaigners, is the low level of *involvement of disabled people* in framing research questions and designing projects. A related point is the complaint that much research does not adequately capture and convey the *lived experience* of people with disabilities, of carers and of non-disabled people working with disabled colleagues. More use of qualitative work to complement large surveys, and more involvement of disabled people in framing research could improve understanding of what is meant by 'barriers' to employment: individual barriers (overcome by training, and so on); systemic (overcome by efficiency improvements, technological changes); relational (overcome by legislation, education and the like); and structural (requiring physical infrastructural changes and shifts in fiscal and social security policy). There is also a need for more longitudinal studies rather than snapshots of the employment position of disabled people.

- There seems to be a need for more investigation of the needs of disabled people in the workplace and the costs to employers of adapting working environments. The assumption is often made that adaptation will be costly but changes might involve relatively minor adjustments rather than the introduction of expensive technology.

- Much valuable work has been done by bodies such as the City University Rehabilitation Resource Centre on issues relating to the management of impairments and mental health problems for employees, and on the experience of people with mental illness in the workplace.[112] There seems to be a need for more research on the experience (factors in retention and departure) and the needs of people who become disabled while in employment. What lessons can be learned from those who have sustained or even enhanced their careers in work? What is the experience of disabled people who have succeeded in reaching senior positions in work? To what extent are those who become disabled while in work subsequently sidelined, excluded from decision-making, demoted or redeployed?

- What are the reasons why disabled people leave work? Is it as a result of financial, employer or health pressures?

- People with disabilities tend to be in work part-time or self-employed to a higher extent than the non-disabled. There seems to be a need for more research on how far disabled people work part-time or self-employed out of choice, and how far these outcomes relate to processes of exclusion. Related to this, there is a need for better information on the experience of disabled people in temporary and casual work.

- More research could be carried out to identify what alternative modes of employment (in the voluntary sector or intermediate labour markets, for example) offer disabled people which bring advantages over the experience of work in the public and private sectors.

- There seems to be a need for more detailed understanding of the barriers faced by disabled people in entering work at the level of specific sectors and local labour markets, and for information about issues such as length of job tenure; career progression; representation within the organisation; reception by colleagues and management.

- What are the attitudes of employment agencies towards disabled people? What barriers exist which prevent disabled people from taking agency contracts (for example, immediacy of staff need versus requirement for specialised equipment)? How many specialist agencies are there? What is the experience of partnerships such as Brook Street /Friends for the Young Deaf that seek to provide effective advice?

- What are the differences between the experience of those with highly visible impairments, those with invisible impairments, those with 'new' impairments (ME), those with impairments that are treated with scepticism by employers (back pain) and those with highly stigmatised impairments (HIV), in terms of access to employment?

- Are there any differences in the quality of careers advice and preparation for the world of work provided by mainstream and special schools? And what are the outcomes?

- How have attitudes among non-disabled people to the needs of disabled people changed, and how do perceptions change as a result of regular and routine contact in integrated schools and in workplaces?

- Information regarding how many working days are lost as a result of people becoming disabled at work is sparse, and government-sponsored research does not always differentiate between those who are disabled prior to employment or working age and those who become disabled during their working life.

- Disabled people from minority ethnic groups, older disabled workers, young disabled school leavers and those who live in rural areas all seem to be under-represented in the research agenda.

- In relation to ethnic minority groups, data are available from the LFS on the extent of disability and analyses such as age group comparisons by ethnic group can be carried out. However, there seems to be a dearth of qualitative research on ethnic minority experience of disability. Some studies have shown that it is likely that socio-economic conditions have led to higher than average incidence of physical impairments and that older black people are more likely to suffer severe impairments than their white counterparts. There are variations within groups, most showing a lower rate among Indian groups.

- What additional problems in seeking work are posed by inadequate public transport provision for people with disabilities?
- How many disabled people have unmet housing requirements which may impede their access to or retention of employment?
- Do incentives increase disabled people's involvement in the labour market? Berthoud suggests that the failure of DWA radically to reduce the claimant count proves that that disabled people are not much affected by them – at the last count there were only 14,000 recipients as opposed to the predicted 50,000.[113]
- Finally, there seems to be a need for research to clarify reasons for the rise in the number of people receiving invalidity and incapacity benefits and its connections with labour market changes. Berthoud notes the suggestion that the rise in invalidity benefit (IVB) and incapacity benefit claimants is due to an excessive relaxation of the rules governing eligibility.[114] He suggests that the trend needs to be considered alongside the other trends of the last 30 years of rising unemployment and lone parent claimants. Two explanations could be relevant. First, that a tighter labour market has meant that the decrease in labour demand has allowed employers to be more selective in recruitment and retention of marginal workers, of whom one group would be disabled people. Second, that there is a growing social acceptance that those with impairments should not have to work should their disability cause undue stress or pain. There is a difference between an individual's impairment and the (in)capacity for work, but this is not clearly defined. There is also the suggestion that because the claimant count for incapacity benefit is higher in areas where the unemployment count is high this is evidence of people choosing the benefit with the highest value rather than on the basis of the intention behind the benefit. But this can again be countered by the tight labour market theory – local employers are also able to be more selective.

Appendix 2.
Leonard Cheshire / OLR research on attitudes towards disability

The aim of the research was to explore attitudes towards disabled people and policy on disability, using a sample of 'opinion formers' drawn from senior people across sectors and walks of life. The survey questionnaire (see page 103) was devised in conjunction with Leonard Cheshire, the National Disability Council and Demos. Fieldwork was conducted by Opinion Leader Research from 17 to 27 August 1999 and interviewing was done by telephone; 105 telephone interviews were conducted with the sample detailed below. The respondents were drawn from the print and broadcast media, business, the civil service, charities, religious bodies, trade unions and higher education.

This appendix summarises the main results. For full details of the research methods and findings, see the report *Attitudes to Employment and Disability: Research amongst opinion leaders*, published by Leonard Cheshire in September 1999. For further information contact John Knight, Head of External Policy, Leonard Cheshire, at J.Knight@London.Leonard-Cheshire.org.uk.

Details of key findings
Views on exclusion
Over three quarters of respondents agreed that disabled people were excluded from full participation in society, and over two-thirds (69 per cent) agreed with the statement that people were unaware of the abilities of disabled citizens. A large majority (88 per cent) agreed with the proposition that disability is 'irrelevant in terms of whether someone can be a useful member of society or not'.

Breakdown of respondents

	Achieved	*Target*
Civil servants	12	15
(Grade 5 and above in range of departments)		
Special advisers to Ministers	3	5
Advertising agencies (Directors)	6	5
Businesses	27	20
(Marketing Directors, Human Resources Directors)		
Media	21	20
(Editors, Programme commissioners, columnists)		
Think tanks	5	5
Trade Bodies	6	5
(eg CBI, Institute of Directors, Local government Association)		
Other opinion leaders	25	25
(church leaders, consumer organisations, non-disability		
pressure groups, academics)		
TOTAL	105	100

Influences on attitudes to disability

It is clear that close contact with someone with a disability has the most direct influence on people's perceptions of disabled people. Respondents cited a wide variety of things that had happened in the last few years that had changed their perception of disabled people, including getting to know a disabled person, media coverage of disability and work by disability organisations and campaigners:

'I've noticed an increasing number of disabled people playing a part in our organisation. This alerted me and broadened my horizons.'

'We had a blind student who was very capable and able to do much more than [we] expected.'

'A friend who became disabled made me understand their needs more.'

'My mother has become disabled over the past few years and I've discovered how inadequate provisions are for the disabled.'

'The very gradual increase in TV coverage (eg Paralympics) shows us what some disabled people can achieve and how amazing they are.'

'More media coverage of the problems of disabled people and what it means.'

'Campaign against government raised issues and created a lot of sympathy for these people.'

Using the definition of disability contained in the Disability Discrimination Act, interviewers found that almost half the respondents have a close friend or family member who has a disability. Over one third work with somebody who has a disability.

However, *none* of our 105 respondents had a disability themselves. This is a striking indication of the lack of penetration of senior levels of organisations across sectors and walks of life in the UK. Ironically, respondents saw all of the institutions and sectors mentioned as having great significance in promoting changes which will create a more inclusive society for disabled people.

Barriers to full equality in the workplace
Exactly two-thirds of respondents work for organisations that have a policy of active assistance on employing disabled people. While 16 per cent said their organisation do not, 18 per cent do not know if their organisations have such a policy. Despite the relatively high proportion having a policy of active assistance, only just over a fifth (23 per cent) felt that there were no attitudinal barriers to full equality of opportunity for disabled people in organisations such as their own. When unprompted, opinion leaders are most likely to think that the main attitudinal barrier to equality of opportunity for disabled people in organ-

isations is that buildings will have to be adapted and additional facilities provided. Twenty per cent cited this as a barrier in organisations like their own.

Ignorance among employers is seen almost equally as large a barrier, with 18 per cent feeling that it is a principal barrier to inclusion. The perceptions that disabled people will not be able to do the job properly, prejudice and that people underestimate the capabilities of disabled people are also seen as key barriers by opinion leaders (16 per cent, 13 per cent and 11 per cent respectively).

When prompted with a number of possible attitudinal barriers, over two thirds of opinion leaders agree that the fact that 'people are unaware of the ability of disabled people' is a barrier to full equality of opportunity for disabled people in their type of organisation (69 per cent). They agree almost as strongly that 'a concern about disabled people needing lots of assistance and adaptations' also acts as a barrier (68 per cent). There is also a high level of agreement that 'people offer sympathy rather than opportunity' (64 per cent).

Markedly fewer people agree with the statement that 'a concern about negative views of customers or clients' acts as a barrier (29 per cent). Opinion leaders are more likely to disagree than agree with this statement, with 40 per cent tending to disagree and 19 per cent strongly disagreeing. Similarly, over three quarters of opinion leaders disagree that 'A concern that disabled people don't work well with colleagues' acts as a barrier to equality of opportunities for disabled people, with over one in five strongly disagreeing (21 per cent).

Disability rights
The opinion leaders register 100 per cent agreement that disabled people should have the same work opportunities as non-disabled people wherever possible, with 90 per cent strongly agreeing with this proposition.

A very high level also agree that disability is an important employment rights and social justice issue (79 per cent strongly agreeing). Similarly, there is emphatic support for disabled children and young people having access to mainstream education wherever possible, (79 per cent strongly agreeing).

Only 18 per cent of the sample of opinion leaders believe that disabled people already have equal rights in this country: over three quarters do not believe that this is the case.

More than three quarters (77 per cent) of the sample disagree that being able to shop and work over the Internet decreases the need to redesign the built environment to promote equal access for disabled people.

Disability legislation
Nearly two-thirds of opinion leaders claim to be aware of their organisations responsibilities under the Disability Discrimination Act 1995 (63 per cent) – although 24 per cent are not aware of their responsibilities and a further 13 per cent are unsure or don't know.

For those who are aware of the legislation, the main responsibilities are most likely to be seen as providing equal opportunities, (33 per cent), adaptation of buildings and environment (32 per cent) and not discriminating on grounds of disability (27 per cent).

Responsibilities are also described in terms of providing access (23 per cent), and more specifically access to facilities (20 per cent) and access to technology (8 per cent)

Importance of various bodies in promoting social inclusion
The government is considered the most important organisation in terms of effecting change with regards to social inclusion for disabled people with 85 per cent of opinion leaders seeing it as very important, and 13 per cent as quite important.

The media are also considered crucial in effecting change, with over three quarters of opinion leaders seeing mass media as very important in promoting the social inclusion of disabled people.

While the vast majority of respondents feel that charities are important in promoting greater inclusion (91 per cent), these organisations are more likely to be seen as *quite* important (61 per cent) rather than *very* important (30 per cent).

Importance of different policies in promoting social inclusion
The policies that opinion leaders are most inclined to see as significant in promoting social inclusion are as follows:

- positive action by companies to employ more disabled people (67 per cent of all respondents strongly agreeing and 56 per cent of business interviewees);
- government funding for adjustments to improve physical access for disabled people (63 per cent of all respondents strongly agreeing but only 17 per cent of civil servants);
- increased integration of disabled children into schools (61 per cent of all respondents strongly agreeing, and 94 per cent of respondents overall agreeing that disabled children and adults should have access to mainstream education);
- 69 per cent of the sample agreed that disability should be included as a core part of the national curriculum's proposed module on citizenship education.

Having a voluntary code of conduct for businesses on disability rights is slightly more popular than legal enforcement orders by the Disability Rights Commission (46 per cent and 32 per cent strongly agreeing respectively). Eighty per cent of all respondents and 89 per cent of businesses supporting a voluntary code of conduct. A total of two-thirds of both all respondents and businesses do, however, support legal enforcement to some extent.

Other measures which respondents say they would like to see introduced to promote social inclusion of disabled people include:

- changes in the benefits system;
- more positive media portrayals of disabled people;
- more disabled people in high profile positions;
- measures to increase public awareness of disability issues.

Survey questionnaire
The OLR questionnaire is reproduced below.

Q1 Which, if any, of these statements applies to you?
- I have a close friend/family member who has a disability
- I work with someone who has a disability
- I have a disability

Q2 Does the organisation that you work for have a policy of active assistance on employing disabled people?
- Yes
- No
- Don't know

Q3 What do you think are the main attitudinal barriers to full equality of opportunity for disabled people in organisations such as your own?

Q4 How much do you agree or disagree that the following are barriers to full equality of opportunity for disabled people in organisations such as your own?
- People are unaware of the ability of disabled people
- People offer sympathy rather than opportunity
- A concern that disabled people don't work well with colleagues
- A concern about negative views by customers or clients
- A concern about disabled people needing lots of assistance and adaptations

Q5 And could you tell me how much you agree or disagree with the following statements?
- Disability is an important employment rights and social justice issue
- Disability is irrelevant in terms of whether someone can be a useful member of society or not
- Disabled people already have equal rights in this country
- Disabled people should have the same work opportunities as non disabled people wherever possible
- Disabled children and young people should have access to mainstream education wherever possible
- Disabled people tend to be excluded from taking a full role in society
- Designing the built environment so there is equal access for disabled people would benefit non disabled people too
- Being able to shop and work over the Internet decreases the need to design the built environment so that disabled people have equal access

Q6 Are you aware of your organisation's responsibilities under the Disability Discrimination Act 1995?
- Yes
- No
- Don't know

Q7 IF YES at Q6: Can you briefly tell me what these responsibilities are?

Q8 How important do you feel the following organisations are in terms of effecting change with regards to social inclusion for disabled people?
- Businesses
- Media
- Government
- Charities
- Education sector
- Scientific institutions
- Religious institutions

Q9 Are you aware that there is now a New Deal for Disabled People specifically aimed at helping disabled people into work or training?
- Yes
- No

Q10 How much would you agree or disagree with the following policies to promote the social inclusion of disabled people?
- Voluntary code of conduct by businesses
- Legal enforcement orders by the Disability Rights Commission
- Positive action by companies to employ more disabled people
- Including disability as a core part of the national curriculum in education for citizenship
- Using disabled people in advertising, TV and films
- More publicity for the existing disability discrimination legislation
- Increased integration of disabled children into schools
- Government funding for adjustments to improve physical access for disabled people

Q11 Are there any other measures that you would like to see introduced to promote social inclusion of disabled people?

Q12 Is there anything that has happened during the last few years that has changed your perception of disabled people? (PROBE FULLY)

Notes

1. Leonard Cheshire, 1999, *Attitudes to Employment and Disability: Research amongst opinion leaders*, Leonard Cheshire, London.
2. Bolderson H, 1991, *Social Security, Disability and Rehabilitation*, JKP, London.
3. Oliver M and Barnes C, 1998, *Disabled People and Social Policy: From exclusion to inclusion*, Longman, London.
4. Ibid.
5. *Disability Briefing*, DfEE, London, August 1999.
6. Ibid.
7. Craig P and Greenslade M, 1998, *First Findings from the Disability Follow-Up to the Family Resources Survey*, DSS, London.
8. DfEE, 1999, op cit.
9. DfEE, 1999, op cit.
10. Meager N et al, 1998, *Employment of Disabled People: Assessing the extent of participation*, DfEE, London.
11. Rowlingson K and Berthoud R, 1996, *Disability, Benefits and Employment*, DSS, London.
12. Meager et al, 1998, op cit.
13. Lamb B and Layzell S, 1995, *Disabled in Britain: Behind closed doors – the carers' experience*, Scope, London.
14. Meager et al, 1998, op cit.
15. Esmond D and Stewart J, 1996, *Scope for Fair Housing (1)*, Scope/Housing Corporation/Tai Cymru.
16. Howard M, 1999, *Enabling Government: Joined up policies for a National Disability Strategy*, Fabian Society, London.
17. Knight J and Brent M, 1999, *Excluding Attitudes: Disabled people's experience of social exclusion*, Leonard Cheshire, London.
18. Knight J and Brent M, 1998, *Access Denied: Disabled people's experience of social exclusion*, Leonard Cheshire, London.
19. Leonard Cheshire, 1999, op cit; see also appendix 2.
20. Oliver and Barnes, 1998, op cit; see also Zarb G, ed, 1995, *Removing Disabling Barriers*, PSI, London.
21. Oliver and Barnes, ibid.
22. Berthoud R et al, 1993, *The Economic Problems of Disabled People*, PSI, London; Howard M, 1997, *Investing in Disabled People: A strategy from welfare to work*, Disablement Income Group (DIG), London.
23. Esmond and Stewart, 1996, op cit.
24. Carey K, personal communication.
25. DfEE, 1999, op cit.
26. Carey K, 1999, *Access to Information*

in the Digital Age: Key issues for disabled people, HumanITy, London.
27. Coyle D, 1997, The Weightless World, Capstone, London; Leadbeater C, 1999, Living on Thin Air, Viking Penguin, London.
28. Burchell B et al, 1999, Job Insecurity and Work Intensification: Flexibility and the changing boundaries of work, Joseph Rowntree Foundation, York.
29. Ibid; see also Sennett R, 1998, The Corrosion of Character: The personal consequences of work in the new capitalism, WW Norton, New York.
30. See also Scott-Parker S and Zadek S, 1999, Disability and Diversity: the business case, Employers' Forum on Disability, London.
31. DfEE, 1999, op cit.
32. Honey S and Williams M, 1998, Supply and Demand for Supported Employment, DfEE, London.
33. Benn M, 1998, Livelihood: Work in the new urban economy, Comedia/Demos, London; Burns D and Taylor M, 1999, Mutual Aid and Self-Help: Coping strategies for excluded communities, Joseph Rowntree Foundation, York; Williams C and Windebank J, 1999, A Helping Hand: Harnessing self-help to combat social exclusion, Joseph Rowntree Foundation, York.
34 Leadbeater C and Martin S, 1998, The Employee Mutual, Demos/Reed, London.
35. Scott-Parker and Zadek, 1999, op cit.
36. Grayson, D, 'Disability in the marketplace', RSA Journal, vol 3, no 4.
37. Scott-Parker and Zadek, 1999, op cit.
38. See Mulgan et al, 1997, The British Spring, Demos, London.
39. Employers' Forum on Disability,

1997, Making Effective Partnerships, EFD, London.
40. Meager, N, Evans, C et al, 1998, Baseline Survey of the Measures in Part III of the DDA, DfEE, London.
41. Meager et al, 1998, op cit.
42. The Grass Roots Group plc, 1998, The Challenge of Disability: Research Report 1 – Is UK business meeting the challenge, The Grass Roots Group plc, Tring, Herts.
43. See DfEE, 1998, The Learning Age, DfEE, London.
44. Carey, 1999, op cit.
45. See also Bentley T, 1998, Learning Beyond the Classroom, Routledge, London; Cara S et al, 1998, The Learning City in the Learning Age, Comedia/Demos, London.
46. See Bentley, 1998, ibid.
47. See Cara et al, 1998, op cit.
48. Ibid.
49. Mulgan et al, 1997, op cit.
50 Lamb B and Layzell S, 1994, Disabled in Britain: A world apart, Scope, London.
51. Scope/NUT, 1993, Within Reach: The school survey, Scope/Coopers and Lybrand, London.
52. MacGillivray A et al, 1998, Communities Count: A step-by-step guide to community sustainability indicators, New Economics Foundation, London.
53. See Bentley, 1998, op cit, and DfEE Advisory Committee on Citizenship and Democracy, 1998, Education for Citizenship, DfEE, London.
54. Leadbeater C and Christie I, 1999, To Our Mutual Advantage, Demos, London.
55. Lamb and Layzell, 1995, op cit; Kestenbaum A, 1998, Work, Rest and Pay: The deal for personal assistance users, Joseph Rowntree Foundation/YPS, York.

56. Howard M, 1999, *Enabling Government: Joined up policies for a National Disability Strategy*, Fabian Society, London.

57. Howard M, 1997, *Investing in Disabled People: A strategy from welfare to work*, Disablement Income Group (DIG), London.

58. Carey, 1999, op cit.

59. Leonard Cheshire, 1999, op cit.

60. See Coote A and Lenaghan J, 1997, *Citizens' Juries*, IPPR, London.

61. Barnett A and Carty P, 1998, *The Athenian Option*, Demos, London.

62. Howard, 1999, op cit.

63. Enticott J, Hurdiss M, Lamb B and Stewart J, 1998 (unpublished), *New Ambitions for our Country: A new contract for welfare – Scope's response to the government Green Paper*, Scope, London.

64. Ibid.

65. Kestenbaum, 1998, op cit.

66. Hirsch D, 1999, *Welfare Beyond Work: Active participation in a new welfare state*, Joseph Rowntree Foundation, York; Piachaud D, 1999, 'Wealth by stealth', *Guardian*, 1 September.

67. Marks O, 1998, *Equipped for Equality*, Scope, London.

68. Lunt N and Thornton P, 1996, 'Disabled People, Work and Benefits: A review of the research literature', paper prepared for Joseph Rowntree Foundation seminar, 12 November 1996; Zarb G, Jackson N and Taylor P, 1996, *Helping Disabled Workers*, DSS, London.

69. Benn, 1998, op cit.

70 Williams and Windebank, 1999, op cit.

71. Howard, 1997, op cit.

72. Bolderson H, personal communication.

73. See Leadbeater and Martin, 1998,op cit, pp 46-50 on this issue.

74. 6 P et al, 1999, *Governing in the Round*, Demos, London.

75. Howard, 1999, op cit.

76. Ibid.

77. Zarb G, personal communication.

78. Railtrack, 1998, *Disability Strategy: a consultation paper*, Railtrack, London.

79. Audit Commission, 1999, *All Aboard: A review of local transport and travel in urban areas outside London*, Audit Commission, London.

80. Ibid; Railtrack, 1998, op cit.

81. Lamb and Layzell, 1994, op cit.

82. The Grass Roots Group plc, 1998, op cit.

83. Carey K, personal communication.

84. Railtrack, 1998, op cit.

85. Esmond and Stewart, 1996, op cit.

86. Walker A, 1996, *Meeting the Needs of the Future: The housing implications of demographic, economic and social trends*, Housing Corporation, London.

87. Leach G, 1997, *Housing Futures*, Henley Centre for Forecasting, London.

88. Esmond and Stewart, 1996, op cit; Brewerton J and Darton D, eds, 1997, *Designing Lifetime Homes*, Joseph Rowntree Foundation, York.

89. Urban Task Force, 1999, *Towards an Urban Renaissance*, HMSO, London.

90. Shonfield K, 1998, *At Home with Strangers: public space and the new urbanity*, Comedia/Demos, London; Worpole K, 1998, *Nothing to Fear? Trust and respect in urban communities*, Comedia/Demos, London.

91. See Worpole K and Greenhalgh L, 1999, *The Richness of Cities*, Comedia/Demos, London.

92. Carey, 1999, op cit.

93. Moore, P, 'Ageing: the lifespan challenge', *RSA Journal*, vol 3, no 4.

94. Carey, 1999, op cit.
95. DfEE, 1999, op cit.
96. Barnes H, Thornton P and Maynard Campbell S, 1998, *Disabled people and employment: A review of research and development work*, Policy Press, Bristol.
97. DfEE, 1999, op cit.
98. Lamb and Layzell, 1994, op cit.
99. Barnes et al, 1998, op cit.
100. Lamb and Layzell, 1994, op cit.
101. Ibid.
102. Knight and Brent, 1998, op cit.
103. Lamb and Layzell, 1994, op cit.
104. Meager et al, 1998, op cit.
105. Meager, Evans et al, 1998, op cit.
106. Hibbett A, 1998 (unpublished), *Discrimination Against Disabled People: Options for defining and measuring 'a*

reduction in discrimination against disabled people'*, Equal Opportunities and Research Programme paper, DfEE, London.
107. Ibid.
108. Cited in Barnes et al, 1998, op cit.
109. Meager, Evans et al, 1998, op cit.
110. Barnes et al, 1998, op cit.
111. Lamb and Layzell, 1995, op cit.
112. See for example, Floyd M, 1993, *Schizophrenia and Employment*, Rehabilitation Resource Centre, City University, London.
113. Berthoud, 1998, *Disability Benefits: A review of the issues and options for reform*, Joseph Rowntree Foundation, York.
114. Ibid.